GRAND PRIX YEAR
1998

Hazleton Publishing

PUBLISHER
RICHARD POULTER

EDITOR
SIMON ARRON

WRITTEN BY
BOB STONE & SIMON ARRON

ART EDITOR
RYAN BAPTISTE

PRODUCTION MANAGER
STEVEN PALMER

PUBLISHING DEVELOPMENT MANAGER
SIMON MAURICE

BUSINESS DEVELOPMENT MANAGER
SIMON SANDERSON

SALES PROMOTION
CLARE KRISTENSEN

PHOTOGRAPHY
LAT PHOTOGRAPHIC

GRAND PRIX YEAR

is published by
Hazleton Publishing Ltd.,
3 Richmond Hill,
Richmond, Surrey
TW10 6RE, England.

Colour reproduction by
Vision Reprographics Ltd., Milton Keynes, England.

Printed in England by
Ebenezer Baylis & Son (Printers) Ltd., Worcester.

ISBN: 1-874557-38-1

DISTRIBUTORS
UNITED KINGDOM
Biblios Ltd.
Star Road
Partridge Green
West Sussex RH13 8LD
Telephone: 01403 710971
Fax: 01403 711143

NORTH AMERICA
Motorbooks International
PO Box 1
729 Prospect Ave., Osceola
Wisconsin 54020, USA
Telephone: (1) 715 294 3345
Fax: (1) 715 294 4448

AUSTRALIA
Technical Book and
Magazine Co. Pty.
295 Swanston Street
Melbourne, Victoria 3000
Telephone: (03) 9663 3951
Fax: (03) 9663 2094

NEW ZEALAND
David Bateman Ltd.
P.O. Box 100-242
North Shore Mail Centre
Auckland 1330
Telephone: (9) 415 7664
Fax: (9) 415 8892

SOUTH AFRICA
Motorbooks
341 Jan Smuts Avenue
Craighall Park
Johannesburg
Telephone: (011) 325 4458/60
Fax: (011) 325 4146

Features

1998 FIA Formula One World Championship

murray walker
foreword

A very warm welcome to *Grand Prix Year 1998*.

It is a tradition for me to look forward to every Formula One season with passionate anticipation and throughout my long career I have never been disappointed by the outcome.

This past season marked the 50th anniversary of my first stint at the microphone – but it was not just that particular landmark which made it so memorable.

The manner in which Ferrari recovered to turn an apparent McLaren monopoly into a thrilling title battle gave the season a competitive edge which provided compulsive viewing. And, away from the main title fight, who will ever forget the looks on the faces of Damon Hill or Eddie Jordan after the 1996 world champion gave the Irishman's team its very first F1 victory at Spa, in perhaps the most dramatic race of the decade?

It was yet another season which promised much but delivered even more – and for me the icing on the cake was the chance to experience Silverstone at Formula One speed, when I hitched a lift with Martin Brundle in the sensational two-seater McLaren.

You can read all about that in *Grand Prix Year* 1998 alongside the many more public highlights of another terrific F1 season. And I know I will enjoy looking back every bit as much as I am already looking forward to starting all over again at Melbourne next March.

Here's to another great season.

It was yet another season which promised much but delivered even more

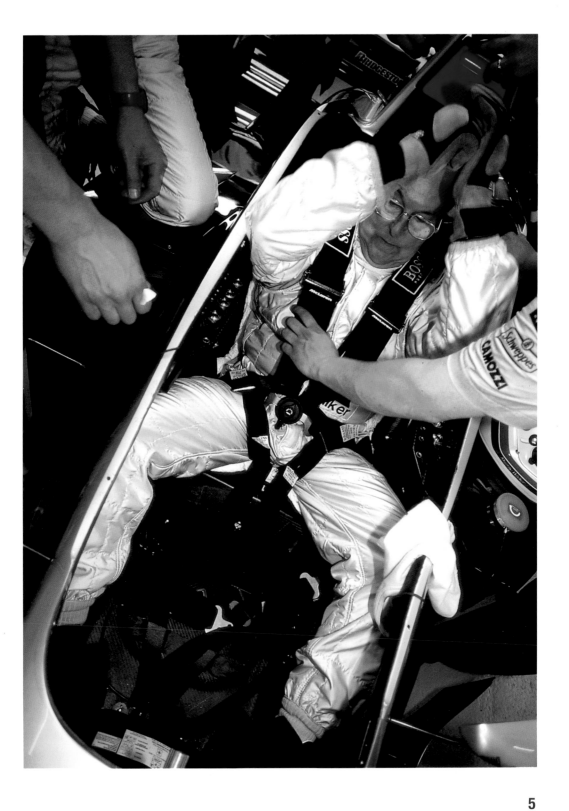

how they lined up

McLaren-Mercedes

DAVID COULTHARD
Born: March 27 1971, Scotland
F1 CV: Williams 1994-95 (1 win); McLaren 1996-97 (2 wins)
Claims to fame: Feet not so much on the ground as buried beneath the surface. Polite, level-headed, honest. . . only slight character flaw is that he admits to liking Aerosmith. That surely can't be why Williams let him go at the end of 1995, can it?

MIKA HAKKINEN
Born: September 28 1968, Finland
F1 CV: Lotus 1991-92; McLaren 1993-97 (1 win)
Claims to fame: It's always a highlight of an F1 weekend when the first post-race interviews are broadcast in the press room and Mika is asked to say a few words in his own language. "Da, grrgrnh dokkadokka hatstand tikkatokka aardvark tukkatukka swordfish." Or something. Even the Finns usually look perplexed

n 1998

from michael schumacher to esteban tuero...some vital (and incidental) statistics about the latest formula one generation

Ferrari

MICHAEL SCHUMACHER
Born: January 3 1969, Germany
F1 CV: Jordan 1991 (one race); Benetton 1991-1995 (19 wins, 2 world titles); Ferrari 1996-2002 (8 wins to the end of 1997)
Claims to fame: Fast. Rich. Expensive. Interviews have to be pre-booked several months in advance (and then you usually have to fly somewhere to find him). Irritatingly good at football. Large collection of pets. Ardent road safety campaigner (particularly since the FIA bollocked him for driving into Jacques Villeneuve in the 1997 finale)

EDDIE IRVINE
Born: November 10 1965, Northern Ireland
F1 CV: Jordan 1993-1995. Ferrari 1996-for as long as Schuey wants him
Claims to fame: Happy as number two to Schumacher – and there are worse ways to earn a living. It's not a job that necessarily brings much in the way of outright grand prix success, but it's enough to keep him in boats, cars, planes and other trappings

Williams-Mecachrome

JACQUES VILLENEUVE
Born: April 9 1971, Canada
F1 CV: Williams 1996-97 (11 wins, 1 world title)
Claims to fame: Famous dad Gilles used to drive the nuts off Ferraris. Reigning world champion. Indy 500 winner in 1995. Started season as a dyed blonde; hair changed to dull purple in mid-season, shortly before he announced that he was to move to the new BAR team in 1999

HEINZ-HARALD FRENTZEN
Born: May 18 1967, Germany
F1 CV: Sauber 1994-96; Williams 1997 (1 win)
Claims to fame: Hired to replace Damon Hill when Williams effectively sacked the 1996 world champion. Used to drive hearses for his father's undertaking business. Sideburns have prospered more than his career since he joined Williams

Benetton-Playlife (a Mecachrome by any other name)

GIANCARLO FISICHELLA
Born: January 14 1973, Italy
F1 CV: Minardi 1996; Jordan 1997
Claims to fame: Highly rated. With barely a season under his belt he became the subject of a tug-of-war between Benetton and his former team Jordan. Loves football, but it is probably indicative of the state of the current Italian side that he cites Paul Gascoigne as one of his favourite players

ALEXANDER WURZ
Born: February 15 1975, Austria
F1 CV: Benetton stand-in 1997
Claims to fame: His dad Franz used to make Murray Walker's tonsils rattle as he was a star of the European Rallycross Championship in the Seventies and Eighties. Alex is a former BMX world champion who wears odd racing boots (one red, one blue). Won Le Mans in 1996

Jordan-Mugen Honda

DAMON HILL
Born: September 17 1960 (and therefore old enough to be Esteban Tuero's dad), England
F1 CV: Brabham 1992; Williams 1993-96 (21 wins, 1 world title); Arrows 1997
Claims to fame: If only his Arrows had held together for another half-lap at Budapest in 1997 that one win would have earned him more credit than the 21 he scored for Williams. But it didn't. F1's senior citizen since Gerhard Berger quit

RALF SCHUMACHER
Born: June 30 1975, Germany
F1 CV: Jordan 1997
Claims to fame: His big brother is quite good. Scored his first F1 podium finish in acrimonious circumstances after barging erstwhile team-mate Fisichella off the road

Prost-Peugeot

OLIVIER PANIS
Born: September 2 1966, France
F1 CV: Ligier 1994-96 (1 win); Prost 1997
Claims to fame: Not only did he win at Monaco in 1996, thereby giving Ligier its first win for 15 years, he did so from 14th on the grid. Showed signs that he could win in 1997, too, until a violent accident in Canada broke his legs and caused him to miss a few races

JARNO TRULLI
Born: July 13 1974
F1 CV: Minardi 1997; Prost 1997
Claims to fame: Named after late Finnish motorcycling ace Jarno Saarinen, of whom his father was a big fan. Said to bear a strong resemblance to Eric Gates, a key member of the well-balanced Ipswich Town squad of 20 years ago

Sauber-Petronas

JEAN ALESI
Born: June 11 1964, France
F1 CV: Tyrrell 1989-90; Ferrari 1991-95 (one win); Benetton 1996-97
Claims to fame: Famed for ability to drive racing cars on bald tyres in torrential downpours and also for his moodswings. Once allegedly locked in the Benetton truck at Silverstone by mechanics who were tired of an ongoing tantrum. More GP starts than any other current driver

JOHNNY HERBERT
Born: June 27 1964, England
F1 CV: How long have you got? Benetton 1989; Tyrrell 1989; Lotus 1990-94; Ligier 1994 (one race); Benetton 1994-95 (2 wins); Sauber 1996-97
Claims to fame: Second to his team-mate in number of GP starts. Similar in terms of experience, opposite in terms of temperament. Son of an electrician. Fan club run enthusiastically by his parents Bob and Jane. Won Le Mans in 1991

Arrows-TWR

PEDRO DINIZ
Born: May 22 1970, Brazil
F1 CV: Forti 1995; Ligier 1996; Arrows 1997
Claims to fame: Dismissed initially as being rich and, frankly, rubbish but has proved his critics wrong with his blend of cash and occasional competence. Scion of a wealthy supermarket dynasty does this because he really wants to, not just because he can afford to

MIKA SALO
Born: November 30 1966, Finland
F1 CV: Lotus 1994; Tyrrell 1995-1997
Claims to fame: The last man to run a full grand prix non-stop (at Monaco in 1997). Where most of his contemporaries spend their money on yachts and planes, he buys CDs. All right, and a Ferrari

Stewart-Ford

RUBENS BARRICHELLO
Born: May 23 1972
F1 CV: Jordan 1993-1996; Stewart 1997
Claims to fame: Spearheads dwindling Brazilian F1 challenge as most of the nation's bright young things seek fame and fortune in the United States. Barrichello has an odd view of retirement. When pressed on the subject, he says he might go off and race in the States

JAN MAGNUSSEN
Born: July 4 1973, Denmark
F1 CV: McLaren (one race) 1995; Stewart 1997; sacked mid-season 1998
Claims to fame: Failure to translate obvious gifts into F1 consistency led to him getting the red card. A future in the States beckons. Since leaving F1 he has had a spectacular tattoo put on his left shoulder

Tyrrell-Cosworth

TORANOSUKE TAKAGI
Born: February 12 1974, Japan
F1 CV: New boy this season
Claims to fame: Reputed to be fast but short on racecraft in his native Japan; arrived in Europe to reveal that he was even shorter on languages. Began communicating with engineers by using a system of numbers to indicate seriousness of understeer/oversteer or whatever. Possibly not great for evolving car set-ups

RICARDO ROSSET
Born: July 27 1968, Brazil
F1 CV: Footwork 1996; Lola (very briefly) 1997
Claims to fame: Former champion triathlete in his homeland. Comes from a family which is big in the lycra business

JOS VERSTAPPEN
Born: March 4 1972, Holland
F1 CV: Benetton 1994; Simtek (until it collapsed) 1995; Footwork 1996; Tyrrell 1997
Claims to fame: Too much, too young? Flung into F1 with barely 50 races to his name. The hype surrounding him once provoked ire from another young hopeful trying to break into F1 at the same time – Paul Stewart, now managing director of Stewart GP. Rescued from messing around at kart tracks when Magnussen's departure created mid-season vacancy

Minardi Cosworth

SHINJI NAKANO
Born: April 1 1971, Japan
F1 CV: Prost 1997
Claims to fame: A cosmopolitan, pleasant young man, he went better in the Prost in 1997 than many expected. But still the only one way he could keep a toehold in F1 was to take a crock of yen to Minardi

ESTEBAN TUERO
Born: Yesterday (April 22 1978), Argentina
F1 CV: New boy this season
Claims to fame: The third youngest driver ever to start an F1 race. Managed to get to F1 without achieving much in any of the recognised training formulae. Compatriot Froilan Gonzalez was known as the Pampas Bull in the Fifties; Tuero is more the Pampers Bull

Hi-ho silver lining: Hakkinen and Coulthard lurk ahead of the field moments from the start of the 1998 season (right). A couple of hours later they were still side by side (above), celebrating their one-two duopoly with Heinz-Harald Frentzen, the fastest son of an undertaker in the F1 business.

race organisers in a tizz after mclaren drivers reveal that they had a pre-race plan and – in a savage blow for the modern sporting code – they kept their word

qantas
australian
grand prix

As he crossed the line to win the Australian GP, Mika Hakkinen could have been forgiven for feeling a sense of déjà vu.

After all, he'd performed the same feat at Jerez the previous autumn, when he was gifted victory in 1997's final race. And as in Spain, everybody was arguing about the way in which he had done it.

Around Melbourne's dusty Albert Park, the Finn and McLaren team-mate David Coulthard simply destroyed the opposition with the new Mercedes-powered MP4/13 chassis. But this was hardly a race.

Such was the level of dominance that there was a pact at McLaren: whoever led at Turn One was to win. So far so good: Hakkinen got the jump on Coulthard as they blasted away to lap the field. But then the Finn bungled by mistakenly heading for the pits at half-distance and Coulthard found himself with a commanding advantage. Until three laps from the end, that is, when the Scot all but parked up and let Hakkinen steam back into the lead.

Detractors wondered how could the team pull such a cynical stunt as hundreds of outraged punters ripped up betting slips that foretold a Coulthard victory.

McLaren responded by caring not one jot. "If we'd have let them race it would have been

hundreds of outraged punters ripped up betting slips that foretold a Coulthard victory

Gone West: Hakkinen and Coulthard peel in after trouncing the rest of the field by over a lap (main shot). There's no sign of any betting slips being shredded in the pit lane, however.

a walkover in the
park

FORMULA One people are bad losers. Wander the ranks of the defeated after a grand prix and you'll encounter scowls, clenched teeth – and even perfectly pleasant people who just don't want to talk to you until they've dabbed off the stain of failure. Fact: nobody in F1 sets out to finish second, even if they have no chance of winning.

But after McLaren's all-silver whitewash, even its most bitter rivals were philosophical – cheerful, even. It was as if, in the face of Hakkinen and Coulthard's crushing superiority, they knew they had no choice but to resign themselves to several months in factories, wind tunnels and at test sessions to close the yawning gulf to Ron Dennis' men.

While naysayers complained that McLaren's brake-steer system contravened the rules, and others suggested it was running everything from trick suspension to performance-enhancing energy-storing technology, most agreed that the MP4/13 chassis was simply cooked up by a bunch of automotive Marco Pierre Whites.

Everyone had seen it coming. Pre-season, this was the car most keenly anticipated – feared, even – by the opposition. The recruitment of ex-Williams design guru Adrian Newey as technical director had galvanised McLaren's engineering strength. It already had, in the Mercedes V10, the most potent engine in F1 – not to mention two of the best drivers.

On the machine's first test run, Hakkinen lapped Spain's Barcelona track a whopping two seconds quicker than his rivals – before, it is rumoured, the team told its drivers not to show their hand.

They saved that for Melbourne. And how. While drivers mostly struggled with their new-for-1998 contenders, sliding and spinning as they came to terms with their reduced levels of grip, it was business as usual for Hakkinen and Coulthard. Their machines looked stable, easy to handle – and visibly quicker than everybody else out there.

Not everybody was bowled over, though. Schumacher, the man last seen planting a size nine racing boost on his stricken Ferrari, talked fighting talk.

"Their advantage is not as big as it looked," he said. "I'm confident we will be up with them, because we are expecting extra performance in Brazil."

Problem was, no one believed him.

Heinz being mean: Several continents behind the two leaders, Frentzen defends furiously to keep Irvine off the podium as Williams finds out what it is like to get a good gubbing (top right). It must have been hot in Melbourne (above right): Alexander Wurz is reportedly so cool that an umbrella would normally be superfluous

sheer lunacy," said team chief Ron Dennis. "We're here to win a championship for the drivers and the team."

He didn't specify which particular driver.

Coulthard kept his cool and pointed out that the team didn't know if the wonderful MP4/13's reliability would hold and that Hakkinen should not be punished for a "team mistake". But there was no doubt that the Finn now owed him one.

Neither was there any doubt that the new McLaren was in a race of its own for now. The only possible rival, predictably, was Michael Schumacher – but although the German briefly stuck his Ferrari's nose inside Coulthard on the first lap he was destined to park with a dead engine. You needed a calendar, not

Ford fiasco: Stewart arrived with precious little in the way of testing and its two cars managed a solitary racing lap. Barrichello walks away (below).

break, rattle and roll

AUSTRALIA was a grand prix whose statistics were unpalatable for every team not wearing a silver-grey uniform, but one nugget of data gave particular cause for concern. By half-distance, when the McLaren-Mercs were about to notch up a minute's lead, half of the field had already retired from the race and the pits resembled a carbon fibre graveyard.

This was a spectacular rate of attrition, but there were good reasons for it.

This year F1 was subject to its most swingeing rule changes since the mid-Eighties, aimed squarely at slowing down the fastest racing cars in the world. Tyres were cut with unsightly grooves to reduce their level of track contact and cars were made narrower and bulkier to interfere with performance-critical aerodynamics.

As a result, the paddock's less well-heeled residents faced a major struggle to get their new contenders out at all, let alone on time – and an even greater one to persuade them to run for more than a couple of laps without stopping in clouds of smoke. This, combined with the demands of a trip halfway round the world to race their creations, left several looking ready to pack up and go home even before the start.

The Stewart pit smelled of burnt midnight oil, the team having arrived in Oz with only one complete car. Their reward for rustling up two more? Rubens Barrichello and Jan Magnussen barely managed a racing lap between them.

Arrows had racked up little more than walking-distance mileage on its own behind-schedule contender, thanks primarily to a bold decision to build its own engine. Team boss Tom Walkinshaw, nothing if not a realist, was treating the season's opening three races as extended tests. Neither of his drivers featured beyond lap 22.

Perhaps the Prost team suffered most, though. Tottering under the weight of French national expectation after teaming up with Peugeot, Alain Prost and his men headed Down Under unsure if they could even use their new car, as it had not passed all of its crash tests.

sophisticated TAG Heuer computers, to time the gap to the rest.

Following Schuey's demise the off-colour Williams team always looked likely to win Division Two, although it was Heinz-Harald Frentzen who prevailed in third as reigning world champion Jacques Villeneuve struggled home fifth.

Two more Brits joined Coulthard in the points once Giancarlo Fisichella's Benetton had been hamstrung by a wonky rear wing: Eddie Irvine was a solid fourth for Ferrari and Johnny Herbert sixth for Sauber. They fared better than Damon Hill, whose high-profile Jordan debut failed to yield much more than midfield tedium.

It was all overshadowed by the post-race news that GP promoter Ron Walker – a man who is to diplomacy what Frank Bruno is to ballet dancing – wanted McLaren in the dock for cheating the fans.

Controversy, conspiracy, acrimony – it was as if F1 had never been away.

Last passed, the Prost: The new Prost-Peugeot had still to complete its crash test programme when it arrived in Australia. Once that hurdle was overcome, the two cars struggled mightily in the race.

When it was finally given the green light drivers Jarno Trulli and Olivier Panis didn't need to struggle too hard to keep their joy in check – because pre-season testing had revealed the AP01 chassis to be a chien requiring a good deal more than house-training.

At least the gutsy Panis took the chequered flag, albeit miles behind in last place.

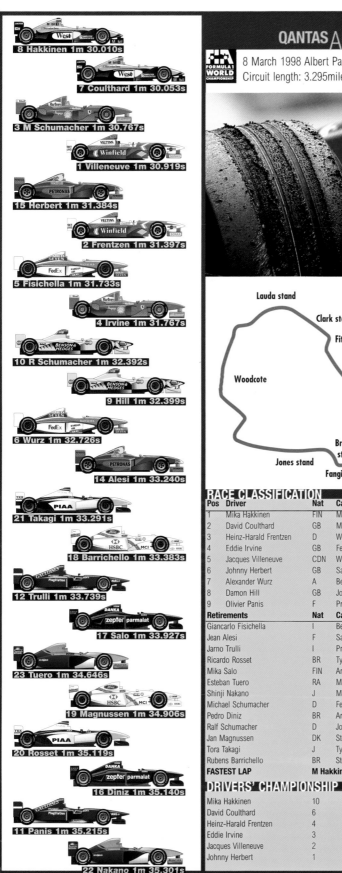

FORMULA 1 WORLD CHAMPIONSHIP

8 March 1998 Albert Park Circuit, Melbourne
Circuit length: 3.295miles/5.303km

Starting Grid

Position	Driver	Time
8 Hakkinen	1m 30.010s
7 Coulthard	1m 30.053s
3 M Schumacher	1m 30.767s
1 Villeneuve	1m 30.919s
15 Herbert	1m 31.384s
2 Frentzen	1m 31.397s
5 Fisichella	1m 31.733s
4 Irvine	1m 31.767s
10 R Schumacher	1m 32.392s
9 Hill	1m 32.399s
6 Wurz	1m 32.726s
14 Alesi	1m 33.240s
21 Takagi	1m 33.291s
18 Barrichello	1m 33.383s
12 Trulli	1m 33.739s
17 Salo	1m 33.927s
23 Tuero	1m 34.646s
19 Magnussen	1m 34.906s
20 Rosset	1m 35.119s
16 Diniz	1m 35.140s
11 Panis	1m 35.215s
22 Nakano	1m 35.301s

Circuit stands: Lauda stand, Clark stand, Fittipaldi stand, Waite stand, Hill stand, Woodcote, Stewart stand, Prost stand, Brabham stand, Senna stand, Jones stand, Fangio stand

RACE CLASSIFICATION

Pos	Driver	Nat	Car	Laps	Time
1	Mika Hakkinen	FIN	McLaren MP4/13-Mercedes V10	58	1h 31m 45.996s
2	David Coulthard	GB	McLaren MP4/13-Mercedes V10	58	+ 0.702s
3	Heinz-Harald Frentzen	D	Williams FW20-Mecachrome V10		+ 1 lap
4	Eddie Irvine	GB	Ferrari F300-Ferrari V10		+ 1 lap
5	Jacques Villeneuve	CDN	Williams FW20-Mecachrome V10		+ 1 lap
6	Johnny Herbert	GB	Sauber C17-Petronas V10		+ 1 lap
7	Alexander Wurz	A	Benetton B198-Playlife V10		+ 1 lap
8	Damon Hill	GB	Jordan 198-Mugen Honda V10		+ 1 lap
9	Olivier Panis	F	Prost AP01-Peugeot V10		+ 1 lap

Retirements	Nat	Car	Laps	Reason
Giancarlo Fisichella	I	Benetton B198-Playlife V10	43	rear wing support
Jean Alesi	F	Sauber C17-Petronas V10	41	engine
Jarno Trulli	I	Prost AP01-Peugeot V10	26	gearbox
Ricardo Rosset	BR	Tyrrell 026-Ford V10	25	gearbox
Mika Salo	FIN	Arrows A19-Arrows V10	23	gearbox
Esteban Tuero	RA	Minardi M198-Ford V10	22	engine
Shinji Nakano	J	Minardi M198-Ford V10	8	cv joint
Michael Schumacher	D	Ferrari F300-Ferrari V10	5	engine
Pedro Diniz	BR	Arrows A19-Arrows V10	2	gearbox hydraulics
Ralf Schumacher	D	Jordan 198-Mugen Honda V10	1	accident
Jan Magnussen	DK	Stewart SF-2-Ford V10	1	accident
Tora Takagi	J	Tyrrell 026-Ford V10	1	spin
Rubens Barrichello	BR	Stewart SF-2-Ford V10	0	gearbox

FASTEST LAP M Hakkinen 1m31.649s lap 39 (129.434mph/208.303kmh)

DRIVERS' CHAMPIONSHIP

Mika Hakkinen	10
David Coulthard	6
Heinz-Harald Frentzen	4
Eddie Irvine	3
Jacques Villeneuve	2
Johnny Herbert	1

CONSTRUCTORS' CHAMPIONSHIP

McLaren-Mercedes	16
Williams-Mecachrome	6
Ferrari	3
Sauber-Petronas	1

Formula One is certainly political. . . but its political correctness is questionable. Still, nowadays pass restrictions are so tight that drivers can only manage one girlfriend at a time (on race weekends). Models do still filter legitimately through the security network, however, as Benetton is no longer the only team infatuated with getting photographers to crowd around its pit at otherwise quiet moments on a Thursday afternoon

glamour
posse

Girl torque – the things to be seen wearing in F1 nowadays (clockwise, from top left):

...A smile...

...A sports bra and a zip-up replica of Frentzen's overalls (unlikely to be a big seller, even in Mönchengladbach)...

...Cleavage in which you could construct a decent scale model of Eau Rouge...

...Glorified Bacofoil (two possibilities pictured)...

...A demure look and a starting position board (the thing on the left with a '5' in the middle)...

...A national flag (amongst other things)...

...Spray-on yellow paint nicked from the Jordan factory.

Holiday Finn: Hakkinen keeps a screen eye on rivals' progress (above), though he could have spent his time just as profitably watching the latest docusoap. He was in a different league to his adversaries all weekend as he annexed pole by three-quarters of a second and screamed away into the distance from the start (right).

mclarens race without disputed brake system but they are still in a class apart as hakkinen scores what many regard as his first true grand prix success

grande premio do

brasil

Going into the Brazilian Grand Prix, Mika Hakkinen's CV boasted two Formula One victories. Interlagos provided his third – but possibly the first which anyone regarded as being real.

Whereas his successes in Jerez 1997 and Melbourne were almost lost in the outrage over clumsily implemented "tactics" which seemed an excuse to gift the Finn some glory, this time McLaren played squeaky clean. It had to because, in a knee-jerk response to Melbourne, motor-

sport's governing body had moved to ban the use of team orders if they were deemed to be prejudicial to the interests of motor racing. This time, as it turned out, Mika didn't need any help.

From the start of practice to the end of the race, nobody had an answer to Hakkinen on the Interlagos track's fast sweeps – not even his team-mate, David Coulthard. Mika had a slight but perceptible edge over the Scot throughout, and used it to devastating effect on race day to streak to an unchallenged victory.

It wasn't quite a spat-free weekend: the

from the start of practice to the end of the race, nobody had an answer to Hakkinen – not even his team-mate, Coulthard

Silver Arrows raced without their controversial selective braking systems, after an enduring protest furore sparked off by Ferrari led to enough stewards' reports to lay waste one of the local rainforests. But McLaren's technological submission made little difference.

By the time the flag fell, third-placed Michael Schumacher was a breathless 30 seconds adrift, his Ferrari painfully lacking the speed to stay with the leading duo despite the German's all-out, race-long attack. But the Prancing Horseman was no more than best of the rest and it was crystal clear that McLaren's domination in Australia had been no

The eyes have it: Damon Hill and Jordan designer Gary Anderson (or at least he was

when irish eyes
aren't smiling

Damon Hill said Interlagos was one of the least enjoyable weekends he'd experienced in motor racing. It was some claim from a driver who has worked for Arrows and the then-dying Brabham team during his grand prix career. But the long faces in Eddie Jordan's normally upbeat camp indicated that he wasn't exaggerating – and you didn't have to look far for an explanation.

The 1996 world champion had gone to Jordan bent on bringing one of F1's most popular teams a long-awaited first grand prix victory. On the evidence of Brazil he stood a better chance of winning the National Lottery. His thunderous post-race expression suggested he was only too well aware of it, and stories circulated that he'd left his team in no doubt about his feelings.

Damon had struggled to hide his disappointment with the 198 chassis from the moment it began serious testing over the winter. Add the fact that he'd joined Jordan after spurning the chance of a McLaren drive, allow to simmer for a couple of races and watch tempers boil over.

If Melbourne was uninspiring, Interlagos was downright disappointing. Ralf Schumacher started the ball rolling by spinning about 30 seconds after the lights went green. Hill – who dropped to 14th after a poor start – lasted longer, but the results were equally mediocre. Both drivers complained of insufficient grip and grunt – and the fact that they were scrapping with Saubers and Prosts rather than F1's Big Four on which the team had trained its sights.

"I was trying to chase Johnny Herbert, but I couldn't catch anyone," complained Hill of a fruitless afternoon's work in midfield. "It was a big letdown." Insiders suggested his comments upon return to the pits had been as colourful as his Jordan's blazing yellow livery.

To cap it all, as Sunday evening drew on the ineffective machine was chucked out of the race results because it tipped the scales underweight at a post-race check. Surely it couldn't get much worse?

then, above) spot a rare species of plover flying past the Jordan pit. Possibly.

Ongrid Birdman: Heinz-Harald Frentzen was slightly outqualified by a Brazilian woman in a swimsuit (far left), but he was best of the two Williams drivers for the second race in succession.

Wurz is best: Benetton's young charger (above left) emerged with credit after his race-long fight with Schumacher (the older, faster one) and Frentzen. He was sandwiched between his fellow Teutons at the flag, in fourth place.

Kerb mauler: Michael Schumacher's natural sense of attack (below left) was enough only to keep him on the same lap as the two McLarens.

racing in **Ayrton's** shadow

IN FEW countries is heroism so highly prized as Brazil. Wander through the shanty towns and slums that surround Sao Paulo's Interlagos track and – if you escape intact – you'll emerge with proof enough.

Four years after the death of thrice world champion Ayrton Senna, the place is fizzing with tributes: graffiti, flags, photographs . . . anything and everything to do with the country's greatest-ever driver. Perhaps it is sheer sentimentality, a reluctance to let go of a sporting god in a country where horrifying poverty is an every-day fact of life.

Or maybe it is just that a replacement has yet to be found.

A nation of massive social contrasts, Brazil has always had sufficient wealth to export a string of talented drivers to the pinnacle of motorsport: before Senna there were Nelson Piquet and Emerson Fittipaldi, who picked up five world titles between them. But post-Senna there was no proven race winner in a top drive ready to fill the late hero's shoes. Fast-forward a handful of years and his home crowd is still waiting – and the point was forcibly rammed home by the fate of the trio of Brazilian drivers on home turf in 1998.

Senna's buddy Rubens Barrichello was the obvious heir apparent, but the Paulista's undoubted potential has been tested more than a little over the years: initially by the burden of Senna's legacy, subsequently by poor cars and unreliability. Interlagos this time provided him with little opportunity to show the flashes of brilliance which have characterised his Stewart career.

Having suffered an Australian GP disrupted by his team's dire lack of preparation, he bounced back to qualify a worthy 13th as Jackie Stewart's men climbed the learning curve of its late-arriving SF2 chassis. The race promised more, as a gung-ho start and a bold single-stop strategy planted him in the top 10, only for the car's still-unreliable carbon fibre gearbox to undo it all.

And Barrichello fared well compared to his monied compatriots Pedro Diniz (Arrows) and Ricardo Rosset (Tyrrell), who monopolised the back row and failed to make any meaningful impression before following Barrichello onto the sidelines, victims of transmission-induced maladies. Rarely did the home fans have so little to cheer.

Senna's shadow still looms large.

flash in the pan.

Ferrari carped rather unconvincingly about how its Goodyear tyres couldn't match McLaren's Bridgestones, although the performance of Alexander Wurz – whose Benetton also used on the Japanese rubber – suggested it might have a point.

The 24-year-old Austrian driver, with all of four grands prix to his credit, scrapped aggressively with Schumacher and Williams duo Heinz-Harald Frentzen and Jacques Villeneuve before reluctantly being forced to settle for fourth. His team-mate Giancarlo Fisichella was more subdued, but he still got in front of Villeneuve as the Canadian looked for all the world like a man still nursing a hangover from the previous October's title celebrations.

But right now it didn't look as though anyone other than McLaren would be partying for quite some time.

Game over payers one and two: Money makes the world go round, according to Liza Minelli, but it doesn't necessarily have the same effect on your car. The well-heeled Rosset (above) and Diniz (right) failed to go the distance in their home grand prix.

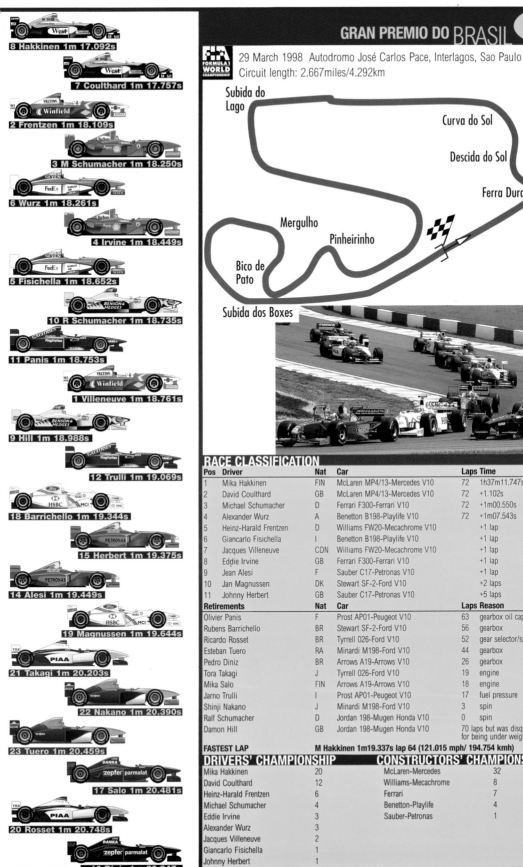

8 Hakkinen 1m 17.092s

7 Coulthard 1m 17.757s

2 Frentzen 1m 18.109s

3 M Schumacher 1m 18.250s

6 Wurz 1m 18.261s

4 Irvine 1m 18.449s

5 Fisichella 1m 18.652s

10 R Schumacher 1m 18.735s

11 Panis 1m 18.753s

1 Villeneuve 1m 18.761s

9 Hill 1m 18.988s

12 Trulli 1m 19.069s

18 Barrichello 1m 19.344s

15 Herbert 1m 19.375s

14 Alesi 1m 19.449s

19 Magnussen 1m 19.644s

21 Takagi 1m 20.203s

22 Nakano 1m 20.390s

23 Tuero 1m 20.459s

17 Salo 1m 20.481s

20 Rosset 1m 20.748s

16 Diniz 1m 20.847s

29 March 1998 Autodromo José Carlos Pace, Interlagos, Sao Paulo
Circuit length: 2.667miles/4.292km

Subida do Lago

Curva do Sol

Descida do Sol

Ferra Dura

Mergulho

Pinheirinho

Bico de Pato

Subida dos Boxes

RACE CLASSIFICATION

Pos	Driver	Nat	Car	Laps	Time
1	Mika Hakkinen	FIN	McLaren MP4/13-Mercedes V10	72	1h37m11.747s
2	David Coulthard	GB	McLaren MP4/13-Mercedes V10	72	+1.102s
3	Michael Schumacher	D	Ferrari F300-Ferrari V10	72	+1m00.550s
4	Alexander Wurz	A	Benetton B198-Playlife V10	72	+1m07.543s
5	Heinz-Harald Frentzen	D	Williams FW20-Mecachrome V10		+1 lap
6	Giancarlo Fisichella	I	Benetton B198-Playlife V10		+1 lap
7	Jacques Villeneuve	CDN	Williams FW20-Mecachrome V10		+1 lap
8	Eddie Irvine	GB	Ferrari F300-Ferrari V10		+1 lap
9	Jean Alesi	F	Sauber C17-Petronas V10		+1 lap
10	Jan Magnussen	DK	Stewart SF-2-Ford V10		+2 laps
11	Johnny Herbert	GB	Sauber C17-Petronas V10		+5 laps

Retirements	Nat	Car	Laps	Reason
Olivier Panis	F	Prost AP01-Peugeot V10	63	gearbox oil cap lost
Rubens Barrichello	BR	Stewart SF-2-Ford V10	56	gearbox
Ricardo Rosset	BR	Tyrrell 026-Ford V10	52	gear selector/spin
Esteban Tuero	RA	Minardi M198-Ford V10	44	gearbox
Pedro Diniz	BR	Arrows A19-Arrows V10	26	gearbox
Tora Takagi	J	Tyrrell 026-Ford V10	19	engine
Mika Salo	FIN	Arrows A19-Arrows V10	18	engine
Jarno Trulli	I	Prost AP01-Peugeot V10	17	fuel pressure
Shinji Nakano	J	Minardi M198-Ford V10	3	spin
Ralf Schumacher	D	Jordan 198-Mugen Honda V10	0	spin
Damon Hill	GB	Jordan 198-Mugen Honda V10		70 laps but was disqualified for being under weight.

FASTEST LAP	M Hakkinen 1m19.337s lap 64 (121.015 mph/ 194.754 kmh)

DRIVERS' CHAMPIONSHIP

Mika Hakkinen	20
David Coulthard	12
Heinz-Harald Frentzen	6
Michael Schumacher	4
Eddie Irvine	3
Alexander Wurz	3
Jacques Villeneuve	2
Giancarlo Fisichella	1
Johnny Herbert	1

CONSTRUCTORS' CHAMPIONSHIP

McLaren-Mercedes	32
Williams-Mecachrome	8
Ferrari	7
Benetton-Playlife	4
Sauber-Petronas	1

this time coulthard had the better of hakkinen – but then schumacher barged in to unseat the scot and give ferrari its first win of the season

Prancing Horseplay: Irvine and Schumacher bear up well to the inevitability of a cuddle on the podium from Ferrari's Sporting Director Jean Todt (above). It was the first sign of the year that Ferrari might be able to inject a little life into the title contest and Schumacher's success was assisted by typically slick pit work (right).

gran premio marlboro de
argentina

They say pride becomes before a fall
– but nobody had told Mika Hakkinen as much.

When asked on the eve of the Argentine Grand Prix how he thought McLaren's rivals would get on, the world championship leader grinned and replied: "They need a miracle to catch us."

It was an uncharacteristic drop of guard and it was swiftly punished by a sucker punch from Michael Schumacher. Down and apparently out after two races, the Ferrari ace fought back with vigour and, for the moment at least, left Mika and McLaren slumped in their corner.

Yet the blows Schumacher landed were more than just psychological.

He hit the front after a robust move which pitched early leader David Coulthard into a fuming spin and left him asking – like Damon Hill before him – for a ruling from the sport's governors on whether Schumacher's tactics were acceptable.

"What he did was not within the spirit of racing and I'll be having words with him," promised the Scot. But his views were swept aside with contempt by Schumacher – as was Hakkinen.

Ferrari's F300 seemed much more at home than the McLarens on Buenos Aires' overgrown kart track and though Hakkinen was able to lead after Coulthard's demise, he was soon overpowered. Put simply, the aspiring world champion was not in the same league as Schumacher when it came to negotiating backmarkers on a circuit where overtaking is harder than it

ferrari's f300 seemed much more at home than the mclarens on buenos aires' overgrown kart track

bust williams

ALTHOUGH Michael Schumacher scored back-to-back world titles for Benetton in 1994/95, Formula One champions have often become accustomed to thin pickings in the year after their title campaign. Ask Damon Hill.

Argentina, meanwhile, showed that Jacques Villeneuve would be no exception.

Pre-season, the ebullient French-Canadian was looking forward to proving that his crown was no flash in the pan and he had every reason to be confident. Natty new red clobber aside, his Williams team was largely unchanged from the operation which had picked up four of the past six world drivers' titles and its new contender was widely acclaimed as a good-looking machine destined for further glory.

Wrong.

In Argentina, the indifferent showings of the first two races gave way to outright mediocrity. Where new Goodyear tyres added zest to a resurgent Ferrari, they only highlighted the work that Williams had to do to get Villeneuve and Heinz-Harald Frentzen anywhere near the top step of the podium. Both struggled to stay on terms with the Benettons, never mind McLaren or Ferrari, and a fraught weekend yielded not a single point.

While critics suggested the drivers should shoulder part of the blame, others pointed to the defection to McLaren of Adrian Newey – designer of Williams' most recent successful chassis – as a more likely cause for its fall from grace.

As it turned out, Villeneuve spent much of the race in pitched battle with David Coulthard's McLaren – but only because the silver machine had been booted back into the midfield by Schumacher. Their dice ended when they clashed and Villeneuve spun into a retirement he regarded as typical of Williams' current fortunes.

"Who knows whose fault it is?" he shrugged. "It doesn't really matter at this point."

Bloodied but unbowed, the team packed up and set off for a private test at Jerez in Spain to look for more performance. But it would be a while before they finally found it.

Beached boy: World champion Villeneuve walks away (above) after his spat with Coulthard.

Steady Eddie: Irvine holds off Wurz (far left). The Austrian only gave up his tenacious pursuit of third place when he spun.

Take a brake: Hakkinen locks up (above left) as he consolidates his points lead with a solid second place.

Grass track: A rare shot of David Coulthard not hitting – or being hit by – someone (below left). Still, at least he's not on the track, which would have been most out of character in Argentina.

is in the Wandsworth one-way system at five on a Friday evening. A late rain shower only underlined the point.

To rub salt into McLaren's wounds, Ferrari number two Eddie Irvine appeared on the final step of the rostrum. The Ulsterman fended off a strong challenge from Alexander Wurz's Benetton after the Austrian once again showed that he had no fear taking on more established rivals – until a spin persuaded him to settle for fourth.

And Coulthard? DC roared back into the pack after the early assault, but he spent the afternoon going round and round in circles behind slower cars. Eventually he and Jacques Villeneuve came to blows after a battle as juicy as a local steak and the resulting spin dropped him to sixth.

One point, he grimaced, didn't amount to much from a race he expected to win. But with Schumacher around, all anybody could reasonably expect was the unexpected.

"I'd say the miracle has arrived," said Michael, dryly.

no jam in swiss roll

Swiss hit: The Saubers of Herbert and Alesi (above) run into each other . . . on their very first lap of the weekend.

Turn-in Japanese: Not all silver F1 cars are dynamite. Even so, the crowd was rooting for the Minardi of Tuero, though it was Nakano (pictured) who made the finish.

IF LADY LUCK seems partial to certain F1 drivers, then equally there are those she wouldn't been seen dead with. Enter Johnny Herbert, rated by many as the most naturally gifted of Britain's four F1 drivers yet easily the most overlooked – despite his two grand prix wins in 1995.

Entering his third season with the Swiss Sauber team, however, the taste of champagne was fading from the Romford man's memory as he faced up to one of his stiffest tests yet: coping with mercurial new team - mate Jean Alesi.

For all their polite PR, this pair seemed unlikely to hit it off. And when they hit each other on their first practice lap at Buenos Aires the writing was on the wall.

But an embarrassed Alesi meekly accepted the blame. "On some mornings it is better not to get out of bed," he said during the build-up to what was one of the least fruitful weekends of Herbert's lengthy career.

After his disrupted practice, the Briton's qualifying session was ruined by brake problems and then a transmission failure – which left him sufficiently enraged to stomp back to the pits and scream at the team's senior management.

The result was a dismal 12th place on the grid which left him fighting Damon Hill's equally evil Jordan during the race. The pair are old sparring partners from the junior formulae but rarely had their battles turned physical.

Until now.

Jordan front wing hit Sauber rear as the pair dived into the chicane. Predictably, it was Herbert who retired while Hill pitted for a new nose.

"I was having a look and he just chopped across my front," complained Damon.

Johnny responded: "If he knew I was there he could have given me room. I'm surprised he didn't, given all his experience."

To cap it all Alesi raced home a strong fifth.

"The only thing left to go wrong is for the plane to crash on the way home," summarised Herbert.

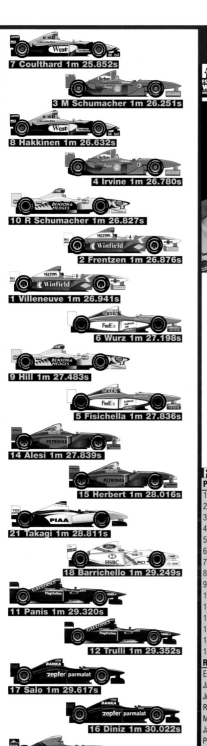

7 Coulthard 1m 25.852s
3 M Schumacher 1m 26.251s
8 Hakkinen 1m 26.632s
4 Irvine 1m 26.780s
10 R Schumacher 1m 26.827s
2 Frentzen 1m 26.876s
1 Villeneuve 1m 26.941s
6 Wurz 1m 27.198s
9 Hill 1m 27.483s
5 Fisichella 1m 27.836s
14 Alesi 1m 27.839s
15 Herbert 1m 28.016s
21 Takagi 1m 28.811s
18 Barrichello 1m 29.249s
11 Panis 1m 29.320s
12 Trulli 1m 29.352s
17 Salo 1m 29.617s
16 Diniz 1m 30.022s
22 Nakano 1m 30.054s
23 Tuero 1m 30.158s
20 Rosset 1m 30.437s
19 Magnussen 1m 31.178s

GRAN PREMIO MARLBORO DE ARGENTINA ⬭03

12 April 1998 Autodromo Oscar Alfredo Galvez, Buenos Aires
Circuit length: 2.646miles/4.259km

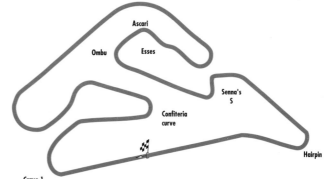

Ascari
Ombu   Esses
Senna's S
Confiteria curve
Hairpin
Curve 1

RACE CLASSIFICATION

Pos	Driver	Nat	Car	Laps	Time
1	Michael Schumacher	D	Ferrari F300-Ferrari V10	72	1h48m36.175s
2	Mika Hakkinen	FIN	McLaren MP4/13-Mercedes V10	72	+22.898s
3	Eddie Irvine	GB	Ferrari F300-Ferrari V10	72	+57.745s
4	Alexander Wurz	A	Benetton B198-Playlife V10	72	+1m08.134s
5	Jean Alesi	F	Sauber C17-Petronas V10	72	+1m18.286s
6	David Coulthard	GB	McLaren MP4/13-Mercedes V10	72	+1m19.751s
7	Giancarlo Fisichella	I	Benetton B198-Playlife V10	72	+1m28.437s
8	Damon Hill	GB	Jordan 198-Mugen Honda V10		+1 lap
9	Heinz-Harald Frentzen	D	Williams FW20-Mecachrome V10		+1 lap
10	Rubens Barrichello	BR	Stewart SF-2-Ford V10		+2 laps
11	Jarno Trulli	I	Prost AP01-Peugeot V10		+2 laps
12	Tora Takagi	J	Tyrrell 026-Ford V10		+2 laps
13	Shinji Nakano	J	Minardi M198-Ford V10		+3 laps
14	Ricardo Rosset	BR	Tyrrell 026-Ford V10		+4 laps
15	Olivier Panis	F	Prost AP01-Peugeot V10		+7 laps

Retirements	Nat	Car	Laps	Reason
Esteban Tuero	RA	Minardi M198-Ford V10	63	accident
Jacques Villeneuve	CDN	Williams FW20-Mecachrome V10	52	accident
Johnny Herbert	GB	Sauber C17-Petronas V10	46	accident/puncture
Ralf Schumacher	D	Jordan 198-Mugen Honda V10	22	rear suspension/spin
Mika Salo	FIN	Arrows A19-Arrows V10	18	gearbox
Jan Magnussen	DK	Stewart SF-2-Ford V10	17	transmission
Pedro Diniz	BR	Arrows A19-Arrows V10	13	gearbox

FASTEST LAP A Wurz 1m28.179s lap 39 (108.043mph/173.878kmh)

DRIVERS' CHAMPIONSHIP

Mika Hakkinen	26
Michael Schumacher	14
David Coulthard	13
Eddie Irvine	7
Heinz-Harald Frentzen	6
Alexander Wurz	6
Jean Alesi	2
Jacques Villeneuve	2
Giancarlo Fisichella	1
Johnny Herbert	1

CONSTRUCTORS' CHAMPIONSHIP

McLaren-Mercedes	39
Ferrari	21
Williams-Mecachrome	8
Benetton-Playlife	7
Sauber-Petronas	3

Coronation Scot: David Coulthard must have spotted a few of his relatives (below) as there was unlikely to be anyone in the crowd remotely interested in a salute from a non-Ferrari driver. A comfortable victory (right) allowed him to forget the trials of the first three races. . . at least for now.

fortune favours the braveheart as coulthard leads all the way, despite a late flurry of panic in the mclaren pit

18° gran premio di
san marino

This was a race David Coulthard had to win – in the eyes of the media, at least. After three grands prix in which he'd freely surrendered one victory and had another forcibly wrested from him, the McLaren pilot could have been forgiven for heading into San Marino feeling slightly queasy.

But if DC was feeling the pressure as the F1 circus returned to Europe it never showed. He led by example throughout, grabbing pole and peeling away into the sunset well clear of the vociferously-supported Ferraris of Michael Schumacher and Eddie Irvine.

Yet his dominant run to victory was only half of the McLaren story. Championship leader Mika Hakkinen shadowed his team-mate early on before slowing abruptly on lap 17 with terminal transmission troubles. And

before long there were anxious faces among the McLaren men on the pit wall as they eyed the telemetry from Coulthard's car.

Late in the afternoon the Scot was instructed to take it easy and he responded by throttling back and short-shifting on the straights. Schumacher, sniffing an opportunity, began lapping at record pace and ripped into what was once a half-minute deficit, but Coulthard remained unmoved, even though the Ferrari had closed to within five seconds by the flag.

But was he really in trouble? Coulthard didn't think so, despite Ron Dennis making increasingly anxious trips in and out of the McLaren pit to

He led by example throughout, grabbing pole and peeling away into the sunset

rich tease

THERE'S nothing like the threat of a Ferrari victory on home soil to mobilise Italy's vast legions of motor racing fans.

Boy, were they disappointed. Second and third places in the race flattered to deceive, because Ferrari never looked like breaking McLaren's stranglehold at Imola. Despite the best efforts of Schumacher, Irvine and their technical department – who rustled up a set of unsightly new wings for the occasion – the Prancing Horses looked sadly in need of a blacksmith. And in light of the latest gossip, that was bad news for Schumacher's employer.

Although he was contracted to Ferrari until the end of 1999, rumours were gathering that a restless Schumacher was being courted by McLaren-Mercedes to get out of his contract – and that he had a clause in his deal to make it happen. Always assuming he wanted to, that is.

Before the race Schumacher met with Gianni Agnelli, boss of Ferrari's parent company Fiat, to discuss his future. Afterwards there were smiles all round, but there remained evidence that the remotest threat of the resident superstar leaving Maranello had set the alarm bells chiming in the corridors of power.

For all Schumacher's claims to the contrary, everybody knew that – without him – Ferrari would have hit rock bottom in 1996, his first season with the team, and that a title challenge would have been out of the question in 1997. And, as Ferrari technical director Ross Brawn pointed out, Eddie Irvine's pace was probably a more realistic reflection of the capability of the F300 chassis.

Ferrari president Luca di Montezemolo was moved to announce that he would stop at nothing to keep its talisman on board.

"We want the best team and the best driver in the world," he said. "We'll do everything we can to make sure that Michael finishes his career with us. How much it costs remains to be seen."

Money didn't seem the overriding issue, however. Already earning over £30 million a year, dosh was never going to be a problem for Schumacher. Having a car that wasn't quick enough after two years of development. . . well, that was another matter, but after the race he was relatively upbeat. "We know exactly what we need to do," he said.

Lone horseman: For passing from one side of this photo frame to the other, Michael Schumacher (above) probably earned as much as the average nurse does in a year.

Last off blast off: A rare start shot without any McLarens or Ferraris evident as Rosset and Nakano keep their fingers crossed that the FIA Mercedes won't outdrag them on the run to Tamburello (left).

check the monitors. The team chief later blamed a "counterfeit" bearing for Hakkinen's retirement – but he admitted in the same breath that he had been fretting unduly during the closing stages of Coulthard's final stint after misreading his data monitor.

Meanwhile, you could almost believe that Williams had misread the 1998 rule book, such was the uncharacteristically poor performance of its car. Big-time revisions were in the pipeline, although Jacques Villeneuve and Heinz-Harald Frentzen at least stoked up morale by tailing the Ferraris home.

"But that was the maximum I could get from the car – it was like a qualifying lap every time," said Villeneuve. "Fighting hard like that just to finish fourth is difficult."

Having been through something similar in Argentina two weeks earlier, Coulthard would have appreciated the French-Canadian's sentiments – but with his title bid back on course, the Scot had plenty of other things to think about.

"It's important that Mika and I are closer on points because that means the focus will be on both of us," he said. "If Mika had built a gap it would be only right that the team focused on one guy."

Clearly, Coulthard intended to be that guy. On the strength of San Marino, he'd built a pretty convincing case. . . at least for now.

wing commanders

Fashion victims: X-wings demurely carried by Damon Hill (above). Still, people used to wear flares – but at least they were cheaper than a few strands of carbonfibre. The FIA banned these wings after Imola, on the grounds of safety rather than aesthetics.

Pass masters: Fisichella ducks inside Alesi (below), though such aggression profited him little. He eventually crashed heavily – though not into the Sauber, which went on to finish sixth.

FORMULA One fashion dictates that there is no such thing as an original idea. Or rather, if you have one, it won't be long before everybody else has nicked it and passed it off as their own.

The early-season fad for mid-mounted aero-dynamic appendages – better known as X-wings, with a nod to Star Wars – was a classic example.

Pioneered by Tyrrell the previous year, the idea of bolting extra flaps to the side of a car in a bid to increase aerodynamic downforce looked positively Heath Robinson in a sport which claims to be more space age than Luke Skywalker. But it had worked for Tyrrell and, with downforce slashed by the new technical regs, plenty of other teams reached for the carbonfibre in a bid to improve their cars.

By Imola, over half the field had either equipped their cars with X-wings or were seriously considering it. And by the time Eddie Irvine wheeled out a Ferrari sporting a pair of horrifically ugly Marlboro-stickered ears for practice, the debate was in full swing: should they stay or should they go?

"If you are talking about banning them for being ugly, then there are a few drivers and team managers who shouldn't be the paddock," said Damon Hill.

Michael Schumacher added: "If ours work, all the fans in Italy will be bolting them onto their Fiat Puntos in the next few weeks."

There was the odd driver prepared to take the matter seriously, however. Like Heinz-Harald Frentzen, who reckoned X-wings were a risk in the event of an accident because they could come off the car and give the driver a nasty bang on the bonce.

As it turned out, Frentzen had a powerful sympathiser: the FIA. The sport's governing body banned X-wings the day after the race – and at a stroke deprived 1998 of one of its dafter yet more distinctive trends.

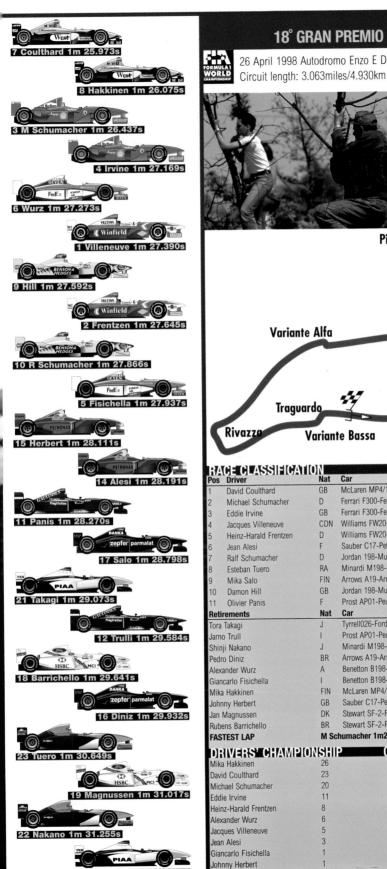

7 Coulthard 1m 25.973s
8 Hakkinen 1m 26.075s
3 M Schumacher 1m 26.437s
4 Irvine 1m 27.169s
6 Wurz 1m 27.273s
1 Villeneuve 1m 27.390s
9 Hill 1m 27.592s
2 Frentzen 1m 27.645s
10 R Schumacher 1m 27.866s
5 Fisichella 1m 27.937s
15 Herbert 1m 28.111s
14 Alesi 1m 28.191s
11 Panis 1m 28.270s
17 Salo 1m 28.798s
21 Takagi 1m 29.073s
12 Trulli 1m 29.584s
18 Barrichello 1m 29.641s
16 Diniz 1m 29.932s
23 Tuero 1m 30.649s
19 Magnussen 1m 31.017s
22 Nakano 1m 31.255s
20 Rosset 1m 31.482s

26 April 1998 Autodromo Enzo E Dino Ferrari, Imola
Circuit length: 3.063miles/4.930km

Piratella · Tosa · Villeneuve · Variante Alfa · Acque Minerale · Traguardo · Tamburello · Rivazza · Variante Bassa

RACE CLASSIFICATION

Pos	Driver	Nat	Car	Laps	Time
1	David Coulthard	GB	McLaren MP4/13-Mercedes V10	62	1h34m24.593s
2	Michael Schumacher	D	Ferrari F300-Ferrari V10	62	+4.554s
3	Eddie Irvine	GB	Ferrari F300-Ferrari V10	62	+51.775s
4	Jacques Villeneuve	CDN	Williams FW20-Mecachrome V10	62	+54.590s
5	Heinz-Harald Frentzen	D	Williams FW20-Mecachrome V10	62	+1m17.476s
6	Jean Alesi	F	Sauber C17-Petronas V10		+1 lap
7	Ralf Schumacher	D	Jordan 198-Mugen Honda V10		+2 laps
8	Esteban Tuero	RA	Minardi M198-Ford V10		+2 laps
9	Mika Salo	FIN	Arrows A19-Arrows V10		+2 laps
10	Damon Hill	GB	Jordan 198-Mugen Honda V10		+5 laps
11	Olivier Panis	F	Prost AP01-Peugeot V10		+6 laps

Retirements		Nat	Car	Laps	Reason
Tora Takagi		J	Tyrrell026-Ford V10	40	engine
Jarno Trull		I	Prost AP01-Peugeot V10	34	throttle stuck/spin
Shinji Nakano		J	Minardi M198-Ford V10	27	engine/fire
Pedro Diniz		BR	Arrows A19-Arrows V10	18	engine
Alexander Wurz		A	Benetton B198-Playlife V10	17	oil pressure
Giancarlo Fisichella		I	Benetton B198-Playlife V10	17	accident
Mika Hakkinen		FIN	McLaren MP4/13-Mercedes V10	17	gearbox
Johnny Herbert		GB	Sauber C17-Petronas V10	12	puncture
Jan Magnussen		DK	Stewart SF-2-Ford V10	8	gearbox
Rubens Barrichello		BR	Stewart SF-2-Ford V10	0	accident

FASTEST LAP M Schumacher 1m29.345s lap 48 (123.433mph/198.646kmh)

DRIVERS' CHAMPIONSHIP

Mika Hakkinen	26
David Coulthard	23
Michael Schumacher	20
Eddie Irvine	11
Heinz-Harald Frentzen	8
Alexander Wurz	6
Jacques Villeneuve	5
Jean Alesi	3
Giancarlo Fisichella	1
Johnny Herbert	1

CONSTRUCTORS' CHAMPIONSHIP

McLaren-Mercedes	49
Ferrari	31
Williams-Mecachrome	13
Benetton-Playlife	7
Sauber-Petronas	4

living the
dream

Take a dream, add three dedicated partners, boundless optimism, openness and an Olympian work ethic.

Stir.

The result would be British American Racing.

Almost a year after the new team was announced at a glitzy launch in London, managing director Craig Pollock has a brand new headquarters, two new drivers, a dedicated staff that grows daily and many months of sleepless nights behind him. With time running out before the season-opening Formula One race at Melbourne next March, it is all systems go.

British American Racing stepped boldly into the Formula One limelight where many other hardy souls fear to tread, fully aware that shipwrecks dotted the shoals.

Setting up a Formula One team is not something for the faint of heart. Try asking Jackie Stewart. Even with his global reputation and a contact book that makes Talking Pages look like a Post-It note, the celebrated Scot admits that stitching together the threads of a Formula One deal was not the work of a moment.

Then there is the case of the MasterCard

british american racing is an ambitious new formula one team which aims to establish itself as one of the best when it hits the track in 1999

the chassis comes from reynard, which has won its first race in every professional motor racing category it has tackled

Lola team, which entered F1 at Melbourne in 1997, on the same weekend as Stewart. By the time the Brazilian GP came around a couple of weeks later, the adventure was over. Others such as Andrea Moda, Forti, Pacific, Simtek, Life, Lambo and EuroBrun have flirted with F1 within the past decade, only to vanish almost as quickly as they appeared. And the majority only ever tasted life at the back of the grid. If, that is, they managed to get on it at all.

Most failed F1 projects are powered by fantasies rather than hard cash. But although the latest Formula One team is the result of one man's dream, its foundations are rock solid.

The ingredients are impressive. Main sponsor British American Tobacco is reputed to have invested up to £250 million over the first five years of the project. The exact figure is a secret: suffice to say that this is a big deal, even by F1's exalted standards.

The chassis technology comes from Reynard Racing Cars, which has won its first race in every professional motor racing category it has tackled – and that includes Formula Three, F3000 and Indycar racing. Reynard has worked on F1 projects before: the last one evolved into Benetton's 1992 Grand Prix contender, which finished second on its debut in Spain. The company now works out of a brand-new 135,000-sq ft factory in Brackley, near Silverstone, and this has been specifically designed to facilitate the F1 programme.

The lead driver will be Jacques Villeneuve, 1997 world champion, a former Indycar king and winner, in 1995, of the Indianapolis 500. He sees sufficient potential in the project to have left Williams, the most successful F1 team of the 1990s, to pitch camp with the ambitious newcomer.

Craig Pollock   BRITISH AMERICAN RACING   Adrian Rey

He is partnered by Brazilian Ricardo Zonta, an F1 neophyte who has won championships at every level he has raced, including the FIA F3000 title in 1997 and the FIA GT1 Grand Touring crown in 1998 with the AMG Mercedes-Benz team.

The V10 engines come from Supertec – a new name for the Mecachrome V10 that started life as a Renault and powered Nigel Mansell, Alain Prost, Michael Schumacher, Damon Hill and Villeneuve to five world titles in six years.

Last, but not least, there is the driving force behind British American Racing: Pollock, a Falkirk-born former school teacher who was Villeneuve's physical education instructor at a Swiss school before he branched out in sports representation and management. He has looked after his former pupil's race interests since 1993.

Pollock says that his F1 project was spawned over the breakfast table at his residence in Indianapolis in 1994. Sharing the

Theatre of dreams: Reynard's new factory near Brackley (opposite) is close to England's motor racing heartland and has been purpose-built for the BAR F1 project.

Driving ambitions: Craig Pollock and Adrian Reynard (above) intend to make their mark in Formula One from day one.

muesli and toast were volume race car manufacturer Adrian Reynard, his managing director Rick Gorne, and Tom Moser, then marketing manager for Imperial Tobacco, now head of Global Sponsorships for BAT.

"We were running Jacques in the Player's-sponsored Indycar team," says Pollock, and the gist of our conversation was, 'Wouldn't it be something if we could move this into Formula One some day'."

Even though he was already successful in business, the prospect of adding an F1 team to his portfolio holds no fears for him.

"It is true, I probably don't actually need to do this," he says, "but this is just the next step in the challenge. It was a dream that turned into reality. I have always enjoyed building up projects and I just have to look at it as another business."

He speaks matter-of-factly, as though he was about to open a corner sweet shop. "It would have been easier to do other things," he admits, "but the fact that F1 is a multi-

43

> ## "if things look to have gone smoothly from our side, it is simply because we have applied a very businesslike approach to the way we have gone about everything"
>
> **Craig Pollock**

million dollar business makes it more attractive to a businessman. Grand Prix racing is a small and exclusive club and it is a great challenge to establish yourself as one of only 11 or 12 members."

In 1999, the Tyrrell name will vanish from Formula One after 30 years. In its place is a bright new organisation that aims to waste little time establishing itself among the best.

From the outside, British American Racing's arrival in F1 appears to have been fairly smooth. In December 1997 the team bought the long-established Tyrrell Racing Organisation, thereby assuring that it would have entry – as well as rights to prize money and TV dividends. This, says Pollock, was easier than starting from scratch – and by the

autumn the sport's governing body had agreed that the team could change its name next year: the cars will be known as BAR Supertecs.

"If things look to have gone smoothly from our side, it is simply because we have applied a very businesslike approach to the way we have gone about everything," adds Pollock. "It has not been 100 percent without dramas along the way, but the hiccoughs we have come across tend to have been thrown up in front of us by the Formula One system, such as the procedure for changing the name. We have had a few hurdles but we have overcome them as we have gone along.

"The most difficult thing, in reality, is getting the key personnel in all the right positions. Without all of them, it wouldn't matter that we had Jacques Villeneuve, Reynard, Supertec or whoever – you have to look at the broader picture.

"You can't come into Formula One by trying

high fliers
behind the scenes

ADRIAN Reynard: founder of Reynard Racing Cars and technical director of the British American Racing team. "I have always said that Reynard would be interested in entering F1 if the circumstances were correct. In British American Racing, we know we have partners who share the same passion for winning that we do. On that basis, we have committed 100 per cent to this project."

Malcolm Oastler: Australian former racer has taken responsibility for designing the first British American Racing chassis. Oastler was the brains behind the successful Reynard F3000 and Indycar chassis which won their maiden races.

Jock Clear: Jacques Villeneuve's F1 race engineer since 1996 is moving across from Williams.

William Toet: Dutch-born, Australian-raised, a keen hill climber who was previously responsible for Ferrari's aerodynamics programme.

to copy existing models. We have studied what has happened to some new F1 teams in the past and we have tried to attain a higher level of professionalism for a newcomer. You can't re-invent the wheel, but you can try to do things so that they work best for all concerned at every level of the organisation."

The team has been running during the summer of 1998. Part of the budget went on setting up a bespoke test team – something Tyrrell has never had – so that British American Racing could gain experience of functioning as a unit. A Tyrrell chassis was adapted to take a Mecachrome engine and former Williams test driver Jean-Christophe Boullion was enrolled to do the shakedown work.

"The first time a BAR-built car ran it was slightly low-key," says Pollock, "because it was a Tyrrell chassis in Tyrrell colours, though the guts of the car were all BAR. I guess the true test of my feelings will only be when we

Strike force: 1997 world champion Jacques Villeneuve and engineer Jock Clear (above) bring a successful and stable working partnership to British American Racing.

get to the first race in Melbourne.". . .

No Formula One constructor has won its first race since Jody Scheckter's Wolf triumphed in Argentina in 1977, and Pollock is taking an entirely realistic view of his team's chances of unsettling the establishment next March.

"I think we will evolve gradually," he says, "but I certainly don't think we will start off at the back. We are aiming to be in the top third of the field from day one and if a driver like Jacques Villeneuve can get into that area, then his racing ability might carry us to victory.

"I know what it takes to be successful and I am willing to work round the clock, seven days a week, to ensure a bright future for British American Racing. I expect the same commitment from the entire team but, at the same time, I hope we can have some fun along the way. We want to be as accessible and open as were are competitive."

45

marlboro de
espana

it was supposed to be a two-horse race, but only one of the mclaren thoroughbreds was capable of sustaining a full gallop. the rest, frankly, were nowhere

Go West: It's conceivable that a load of West Brom fans in the McLaren camp have just heard of a goal at The Hawthorns via Radio 5 Live, or perhaps it was a fourth victory of the year which was cause for such celebration (left). This was the only time all afternoon that Schumacher came close to the McLaren drivers (above).

It's not often that one driver compliments another, let alone bows down in the face of his abject superiority. But given his team-mate's total domination of the Spanish Grand Prix, maybe David Coulthard felt he had no choice.

The Scot had latched onto Mika Hakkinen's tail in the title race by winning two weeks

Michael blamed his tyres and Ferrari technical chief Ross Brawn said the whole package simply wasn't good enough

stewart
makes its point

FOR the most part, 1998 was hard work for Stewart Grand Prix. But at least it could look back on Spain with a wide smile on its corporate face.

Coming into the race, the tartan team which had made such a colourful splash in 1997, its debut year, was on the ropes. It had been set back by the late arrival of its car with its convoluted carbon fibre gearbox casing – an idea too radical, said some engineers, for a team still learning about F1. Equally, high expectations – the result of a stupendous second place at Monaco in its fifth-ever

grand prix – had taken their toll. One year on, Stewart had failed to make discernible progress.

The situation was hardly radical, given the team's youth, but engine supplier Ford was said to be disenchanted with progress and, ominously, was rumoured to be investigating its options for the future. Second driver Jan Magnussen was floundering, low on confidence and widely rumoured to be on the point of replacement. In the media, too, the critics were out in force – but they were abruptly silenced when Jackie Stewart's men hit form at Barcelona.

Although he was undoubtedly assisted by sticky, grippy Bridgestone tyres, there was a lot more than that to Rubens Barrichello's gritty run to fifth (left). Barcelona might make for boring racing, but it is hard on drivers. Anything not absolutely au point on a car is brutally punished by high-speed corners and

earlier at Imola, but now the Finn appeared to have jumped into his passenger seat with a clipboard.

"Mika gave me a bit of a driving lesson this weekend," admitted Coulthard. "I was struggling to get confidence though I hoped that I could overtake him at the start and improve my car's balance during the race by luck. But neither happened."

Nobody looked like getting any change out of Hakkinen all weekend. The lead McLaren driver controlled proceedings from practice onwards, romping to a clear pole position and blitzing his team-mate on Sunday afternoon. The championship leader protested that it hadn't been easy, though that was certainly how it looked.

"It was enjoyable and also quite demanding," he admitted afterwards, flushed with success. "You have to make sure your concentration

Art of glass: Snazzy greenhouse architecture of the Barcelona pit complex allows photographers to capture that vital moment as the Ferrari pit crew comes to the conclusion that they are knackered this weekend. It's a feeling with which the passing Heinz-Harald Frentzen has been all too familiar during his time at Williams (far left).

an abrasive surface. Having the world champion parked up your gearbox for most of the race does not help. But Barrichello – who seems ever destined to be one of grand prix racing's most underrated performers – never cracked.

"We needed this, especially post-Imola," admitted Jackie Stewart afterwards. "Rubens' drive was great, although I don't feel we've turned the corner yet. We've been running behind since Australia, but everybody has made a terrific effort and we know the basic stuff is right now."

Clearly, however, fine-tuning was necessary. Although the team scored points again in Canada, this was a season of toil in obscurity, occasional heartache and little reward.

Exactly what Stewart himself had always said it would be, in fact.

In the frame: There aren't too many pictures of an Arrows in *Grand Prix Year 98*. . . and this one only appears to have made it because Mika Salo is wearing a particularly sharp pair of shades (above left). The Finn is an avid collector of expensive eye furniture.

passing the (big)
bucks

OVERTAKING opportunities in F1 are like pay rises: once a driver gets a whiff, they tend not to let go.

Passing was harder than ever in 1998, so when Giancarlo Fisichella – desperate to keep Michael Schumacher behind him – found himself trapped behind Eddie Irvine, it provoked a battle that always looked likely to end in acrimony.

Predictably enough, it did.

Having zig-zagged all over the straight behind the Ferrari, Fisichella gritted his teeth and boldly attempted to hold the outside line at the first corner on lap 29. Irvine wasn't having any of it and stayed exactly where he was. Result: they collided, piled into the gravel and were soon out of their stricken machines and face-to-face in theatrical confrontation.

"I asked him if he was an idiot," said Fisichella. "The race should have been over on the last lap, not the 28th. I wonder why he seems to have problems with everybody."

Irvine, as is customary, wasn't about to lose any sleep over it. "Oh, he was just telling me I was not correct and all that – typical Italian stuff," he said airily. "He just came straight across to my side of the road. I got hard on the brakes to avoid a collision but, as far as I'm concerned, he just turned straight in on me."

As far as the FIA's stewards were concerned, Irvine had a point. Fisichella found himself up before the beak and fined $7,500 (about £4,500) for "causing an avoidable collision".

Er, hang on a minute. Isn't this the same FIA which has studied ways of increasing overtaking opportunities? The very governing body which admitted it was acceptable for drivers to risk "limb but not life" in pursuit of their Holy Grail? Surely all Fisichella was trying to do was overtake at the one place where such things are possible within Barcelona's godawful configuration? So why was he penalised because it went wrong?

There was widespread sympathy for Fisichella's plight afterwards – and not just from his own team members: even Irvine appeared to feel for his adversary.

"I think it's right the FIA takes action to recognise who is at fault, but I feel sorry for Giancarlo because the fine is so steep," he said.

Bet that cheered the Italian up.

Compared to the McLarens, everybody else looked strictly second rate. That included the Ferraris of Michael Schumacher and Eddie Irvine

All by myself: Jacques Villeneuve plods on to sixth place in the weary knowledge that last year's world title-winning combo is no longer fast enough to keep up with a Stewart.

is right all the way through the race and be careful overtaking the backmarkers." Of which there were many.

Compared to the McLarens, everybody else looked strictly second rate. That included the Ferraris of Michael Schumacher and Eddie Irvine, hamstrung by poorly-performing Goodyear tyres. Bridgestone's advantage was such that it allowed Benetton and – gasp – Stewart to challenge for points.

Schumacher finally came through to finish third, despite a stop-go penalty from the paddock police for speeding in the pit lane. But the silk purse/sow's ear factor would have

been diminished had Fisichella's Benetton not been eliminated in a controversial collision with Irvine. Even so, Schumacher deserved nothing but credit for a barnstorming charge that took him past the second Benetton of Alex Wurz in the closing stages.

Michael blamed his tyres and Ferrari technical chief Ross Brawn said the whole package simply wasn't good enough. But the potency of Bridgestone's rubber bullets was underlined by the way Rubens Barrichello's Stewart – which had handled vaguely like a supermarket trolley at Imola a fortnight earlier – held off Jacques Villeneuve's Williams.

Behind Villeneuve, Johnny Herbert harboured dreams of his second point of the season for Sauber, but he could never stay in the Williams' slipstream long enough to capitalise.

"I lost any chance of points at the start," he said. "Last season I was always one of the best off the line, but this year it hasn't really clicked."

For Hakkinen, on the other hand, absolutely everything had.

8 Hakkinen 1m 20.262s

7 Coulthard 1m 20.996s

3 M Schumacher 1m 21.785s

5 Fisichella 1m 21.894s

6 Wurz 1m 21.965s

4 Irvine 1m 22.350s

15 Herbert 1m 22.794s

9 Hill 1m 22.835s

18 Barrichello 1m 22.860s

1 Villeneuve 1m 22.885s

10 R Schumacher 1m 22.927s

11 Panis 1m 22.963s

2 Frentzen 1m 23.197s

14 Alesi 1m 23.327s

16 Diniz 1m 23.704s

12 Trulli 1m 23.748s

17 Salo 1m 23.887s

19 Magnussen 1m 24.112s

23 Tuero 1m 24.265s

22 Nakano 1m 24.538s

21 Takagi 1m 24.722s

Did not qualify
20 Rosset BR
Tyrrell 026-Ford V10 1m 25.946s

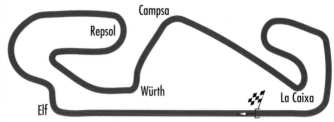

10 May 1998 Circuit de Catalunya, Montmelo, Barcelona
Circuit length: 2.938miles/4.728km

RACE CLASSIFICATION

Pos	Driver	Nat	Car	Laps	Time
1	Mika Hakkinen	FIN	McLaren MP4/13-Mercedes V10	65	1h33m37.621s
2	David Coulthard	GB	McLaren MP4/13-Mercedes V10	65	+9.439s
3	Michael Schumacher	D	Ferrari F300-Ferrari V10	65	+47.095s
4	Alexander Wurz	A	Benetton B198-Playlife V10	65	+1m02.538s
5	Rubens Barrichello	BR	Stewart SF-2-Ford V10		+1 lap
6	Jacques Villeneuve	CDN	Williams FW20-Mecachrome V10		+1 lap
7	Johnny Herbert	GB	Sauber C17-Petronas V10		+1 lap
8	Heinz-Harald Frentzen	D	Williams FW20-Mecachrome V10		+2 laps
9	Jarno Trulli	I	Prost AP01-Peugeot V10		+2 laps
10	Jean Alesi	F	Sauber C17-Petronas V10		+2 laps
11	Ralf Schumacher	D	Jordan 198-Mugen Honda V10		+2 laps
12	Jan Magnussen	DK	Stewart SF-2-Ford V10		+2 laps
13	Tora Takagi	J	Tyrrell 026-Ford V10		+2 laps
14	Shinji Nakano	J	Minardi M198-Ford V10		+2 laps
15	Esteban Tuero	RA	Minardi M198-Ford V10		+2 laps
16	Olivier Panis	F	Prost AP01-Peugeot V10		+5 laps

Retirements		Nat	Car	Laps	Reason
Damon Hill		GB	Jordan 198-Mugen Honda V10	46	engine
Eddie Irvine		GB	Ferrari F300-Ferrari V10	28	accident
Giancarlo Fisichella		I	Benetton B198-Playlife V10	28	accident
Mika Salo		FIN	Arrows A19-Arrows V10	21	engine
Pedro Diniz		BR	Arrows A19-Arrows V10	20	engine

FASTEST LAP M Hakkinen 1m24.275s lap 25 (125.497mph/201.967kmh)

DRIVERS' CHAMPIONSHIP

Mika Hakkinen	36
David Coulthard	29
Michael Schumacher	24
Eddie Irvine	11
Alexander Wurz	9
Heinz-Harald Frentzen	8
Jacques Villeneuve	6
Jean Alesi	3
Rubens Barrichello	2
Giancarlo Fisichella	1
Johnny Herbert	1

CONSTRUCTORS' CHAMPIONSHIP

McLaren-Mercedes	65
Ferrari	35
Williams-Mecachrome	14
Benetton-Playlife	10
Sauber-Petronas	4
Stewart-Ford	2

Crew Alexander: Wonder if this lot supported Wurz as fervently when he was on his way to being BMX champion of the world?

Formula One continues to enjoy an expanding audience, both on TV and in the flesh. Except in France, that is, where in 1998 punters were outnumbered by vacant plastic chairs. But, as you might have noticed, none of these pictures were taken at Magny-Cours

crowded house

Banner in the works: Colossal Ferrari bunting is prevalent at the two Italian races – and however many there are in Germany. Nürburgring and Hockenheim certainly count. . . and Belgium, Austria and Hungary are so close that they might as well be German, too. The races in these countries are very bad news for vegetarians, incidentally.

Sign of the times: Fans froth at the mouth given a rare opportunity to meet King David of Twynholm.

Hilly the kid: Even qualifying in an average position somewhere in the lower reaches of the top 10 is enough to inspire devotion. The win at Spa probably helped, mind.

Twin peeks: Unable to afford TV's pay-per-view boxing charges, fans cluster to the McLaren garage on the off-chance that Michael Schumacher might be trying to punch someone inside.

Grandstand view: Unusual shot of sensible Monza race fans standing on something concrete with a safety barrier at the front. Those without the means for this sort of thing normally make do with climbing trees.

Flagging: It will take a population explosion in Helsinki to rustle up enough Finns to produce a show of support on a Schuey/Ferrari scale.

Top hat: Some Schuey fans can be a model of devotion. . . without going the whole hog and having their hair dyed scarlet.

grand prix de
monaco

Clash of the Teutons: Yes, yes, Mika, you can put your nice, shiny trophies away. While the winner celebrated with Fisichella and Irvine (below), the main talking point was Alexander Wurz's heroic refusal to cede to some bully boy in a Ferrari (main shot).

hakkinen makes it four out of six while schuey shows that theories can be cobblers by failing to cut the mustard at the circuit which suits him above all others

Such is Mika Hakkinen's general post-race demeanour that he runs the risk of appearing . . . well, not dull – but not the sort of bloke you'd take down the pub for an evening chat.

The language barrier, slight awkwardness in front of a room full of strangers and the sheer exertion of piloting a racing car for a couple of hours usually take their toll on the amiable Finn. Monaco, however, was different.

Like most grand prix drivers, Hakkinen calls Monte Carlo home – and the grand prix he most wanted to win. But you sensed that his victory here marked the shifting into place of the final pieces of the jigsaw which turn a fine driver into a likely world champion. It was as if Mika felt it, too, because afterwards he was relaxed and eloquent enough to take on Alan Partridge.

You would never have guessed that he very nearly threw it all away.

jordan **united** in despair

MANCHESTER United football star Ryan Giggs (left) was a guest of Jordan Grand Prix in Monaco, prompting the paddock gag of the weekend: at last there was someone in the team who could take corners.

Laugh? Eddie Jordan's men nearly didn't. Monaco marked the nadir of a season which had started badly and got worse ever since.

Having cheerfully taken the rise out of Minardi before the race, Damon Hill ended it with Shinji Nakano's Italian machine tenaciously nipping at his heels – a fate almost embarrassing enough to persuade yacht-loving boss Jordan to weigh anchor in the harbour and sail off into the deep blue yonder.

Jordan's problems were manyfold. His car plainly wasn't working, multi-million pound signing Hill wasn't proving to be the Alan Shearer he needed – indeed, there was talk of a post-race shouting match between lead driver and his gaffer – and sidekick Ralf Schumacher was still conducting too many intimate searches of tyre walls and gravel traps. The net result was no points whatsoever, much less any prizes, and widespread rumours that Jordan wanted to sell his team to Honda.

For all the ills, however, EJ is more stoic than his habitual blarney might suggest. Escapism certainly was not on his mind.

"There really are no excuses," admitted the Irishman. "I can't fault the drivers, but I know we need to do a lot of thinking. We're going to have a lot more pain before it gets any better."

the boot is on the other schu

Barrier grief: Although Hakkinen looked in complete control all weekend (far left), the Finn admitted afterwards that he had smitten a guardrail hard enough to believe that his race was over. His suspension appeared not to notice his mistake, however, and hence he swept on to victory.

Slings and Arrows: In the tight confines of Monaco Tom Walkinshaw found that both his allegedly underpowered cars were catapulted into the top six. For Mika Salo (left) there was the consolation of a first points finish since this race in 1997.

Alexander the grate: That early attempt to repel Michael Schumacher proved costly for Wurz, whose car subsequently broke in the tunnel and pitched him violently into the Armco. The resulting accident lasted almost all the way to Nice but, happily, the Benetton starlet was shaken, not stirred (above right).

OVER the years Michael Schumacher has made Monaco his playground. A natural heir to the likes of Prost and Senna, he has controlled proceedings at the principality and made it look easy to blasting a 750bhp grand prix car around a track that resembles a multi-storey car park access lane.

There is no doubt, though, that he'll want to forget the 1998 race as soon as possible.

It wasn't that the German was off his game particularly, more that his habitual knack of putting himself in the right place at the right time had deserted him for the weekend.

He completed few practice laps after a crash in Casino Square and subsequent transmission problems. As a result, qualifying was a mountain to climb and, despite gamely attaching his crampons, he was behind Fisichella's Benetton on the grid (as well as the McLarens, obviously).

This ultimately compromised his chances on Sunday and they finally disappeared when he damaged his Ferrari's suspension while battling with Fisichella's firebrand team-mate Alexander Wurz. But pundits were quick to note the symbolic overtones of the two Teutons' wheel-rubbing antics. Here, they argued, was a pretender to Schumacher's crown throwing down the gauntlet to the king and challenging him in his own backyard. Or, as one seasoned observer put it, like Schuey meeting himself coming the other way up a one-way street.

Whether Michael saw things this way is debatable as he returned to the track several laps down, but there was definitely something out of character in his gauche attempt to pass Diniz at the chicane on the last lap. It was not a move which would have gained him a place and it served no purpose other than to inflict more damage to his F300 against the barriers.

It was the ill-judged action of a rookie rather than a champion and it put the tin lid on a very bad day at the office.

Jordan's detractors argue that he is good with words but not so hot on deeds; indeed, his post-race threat to "take an axe" to problem areas within the team was taken with a pinch of salt by most. But, in the weeks following Monaco, technical director Gary Anderson would be confined to the backroom to work on solutions to the 198's poor aerodynamics, Tyrrell designer Mike Gascoyne would be poached to work alongside him and, judging by the rapidity of the improvements, Mugen-Honda's chemistry set would be pressed into useful service.

But that was all in the future. On a stuffy Sunday in Monte Carlo, EJ didn't need Giggsy around to remind him that he was lucky he didn't have a board and chairman to answer to. "Usually in this situation you'd sack the boss," reflected Jordan. "But that's me," he added, "so it won't be happening."

the ferrari man got ahead of fisichella in the pits, but found wurz a tougher nut to crack at the loews hairpin

Hakkinen's victory seemed a certainty once McLaren team-mate David Coulthard retired with a blown Mercedes V10. Title rival Michael Schumacher was bottled up behind Giancarlo Fisichella's Benetton and nobody else constituted a serious threat. Yet moments before a pit stop Mika was caught out by the change of surface at the tricky Rascasse corner – and he thumped a barrier hard enough to make him think it was all over.

But it wasn't. "Thanks to the boys who woke up early this morning to build me nice strong suspension," he grinned sheepishly afterwards.

In fairness, it was the only slip-up of the weekend for Hakkinen as he cleaned up comprehensively. Besides, he wasn't the only driver to check out Monaco's unyielding barriers. Fisichella blotted his otherwise impeccable copybook with a similar mistake at Rascasse, but recovered from the subsequent spin to post a fine second for the resurgent Benetton.

He could thank young gun team-mate Alexander Wurz for seeing off the menace of Schumacher (the older one), however. The Ferrari man got ahead of Fisichella in the pits, but found Wurz a tougher nut to crack at the Loews hairpin. The Austrian banged wheels with his rival before holding his position, while Schumacher headed to the pits for repairs which ruled him out of contention.

Wurz probably wished he had done the same when his impressive drive concluded with a massive accident which started in the tunnel and finished somewhere close to the harbour.

His demise allowed a couple of surprise faces into the top six – including Arrows drivers Mika Salo and Pedro Diniz, whose underpowered machines were a perfect foil for the circuit's tight confines. Salo in particular seemed inspired, fighting tooth-and-nail with Jean Alesi's Sauber and looking as hungry as you'd expect for a man who'd not had a sniff of a point for precisely one year.

But it was another Mika who took the lion's share of the plaudits – and points.

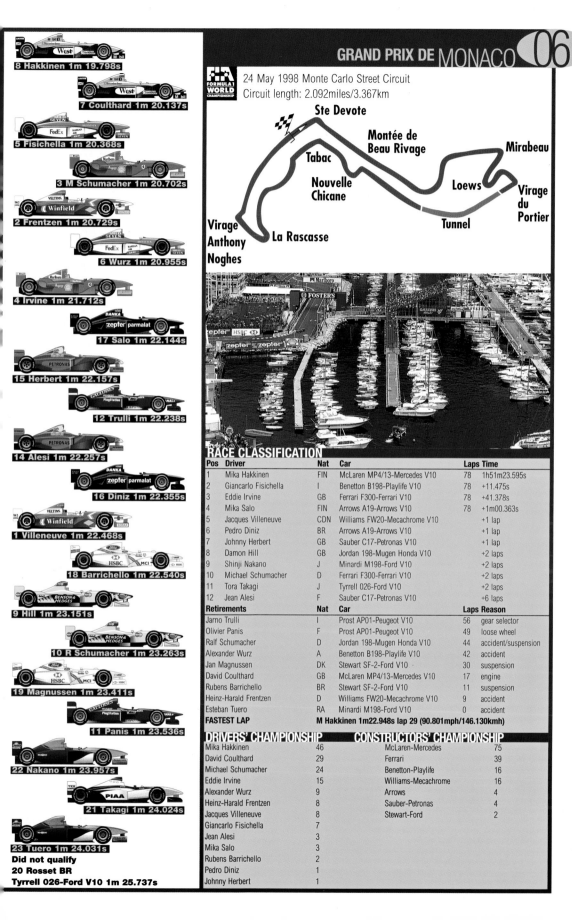

8 Hakkinen 1m 19.798s
7 Coulthard 1m 20.137s
5 Fisichella 1m 20.368s
3 M Schumacher 1m 20.702s
2 Frentzen 1m 20.729s
6 Wurz 1m 20.955s
4 Irvine 1m 21.712s
17 Salo 1m 22.144s
15 Herbert 1m 22.157s
12 Trulli 1m 22.238s
14 Alesi 1m 22.257s
16 Diniz 1m 22.355s
1 Villeneuve 1m 22.468s
18 Barrichello 1m 22.540s
9 Hill 1m 23.151s
10 R Schumacher 1m 23.263s
19 Magnussen 1m 23.411s
11 Panis 1m 23.536s
22 Nakano 1m 23.957s
21 Takagi 1m 24.024s
23 Tuero 1m 24.031s
Did not qualify
20 Rosset BR
Tyrrell 026-Ford V10 1m 25.737s

24 May 1998 Monte Carlo Street Circuit
Circuit length: 2.092miles/3.367km

Ste Devote
Montée de Beau Rivage
Mirabeau
Tabac
Nouvelle Chicane
Loews
Virage du Portier
Virage Anthony Noghes
La Rascasse
Tunnel

RACE CLASSIFICATION

Pos	Driver	Nat	Car	Laps	Time
1	Mika Hakkinen	FIN	McLaren MP4/13-Mercedes V10	78	1h51m23.595s
2	Giancarlo Fisichella	I	Benetton B198-Playlife V10	78	+11.475s
3	Eddie Irvine	GB	Ferrari F300-Ferrari V10	78	+41.378s
4	Mika Salo	FIN	Arrows A19-Arrows V10	78	+1m00.363s
5	Jacques Villeneuve	CDN	Williams FW20-Mecachrome V10		+1 lap
6	Pedro Diniz	BR	Arrows A19-Arrows V10		+1 lap
7	Johnny Herbert	GB	Sauber C17-Petronas V10		+1 lap
8	Damon Hill	GB	Jordan 198-Mugen Honda V10		+2 laps
9	Shinji Nakano	J	Minardi M198-Ford V10		+2 laps
10	Michael Schumacher	D	Ferrari F300-Ferrari V10		+2 laps
11	Tora Takagi	J	Tyrrell 026-Ford V10		+2 laps
12	Jean Alesi	F	Sauber C17-Petronas V10		+6 laps

Retirements		Nat	Car	Laps	Reason
Jarno Trulli		I	Prost AP01-Peugeot V10	56	gear selector
Olivier Panis		F	Prost AP01-Peugeot V10	49	loose wheel
Ralf Schumacher		D	Jordan 198-Mugen Honda V10	44	accident/suspension
Alexander Wurz		A	Benetton B198-Playlife V10	42	accident
Jan Magnussen		DK	Stewart SF-2-Ford V10	30	suspension
David Coulthard		GB	McLaren MP4/13-Mercedes V10	17	engine
Rubens Barrichello		BR	Stewart SF-2-Ford V10	11	suspension
Heinz-Harald Frentzen		D	Williams FW20-Mecachrome V10	9	accident
Esteban Tuero		RA	Minardi M198-Ford V10	0	accident

FASTEST LAP M Hakkinen 1m22.948s lap 29 (90.801mph/146.130kmh)

DRIVERS' CHAMPIONSHIP

Mika Hakkinen	46
David Coulthard	29
Michael Schumacher	24
Eddie Irvine	15
Alexander Wurz	9
Heinz-Harald Frentzen	8
Jacques Villeneuve	8
Giancarlo Fisichella	7
Jean Alesi	3
Mika Salo	3
Rubens Barrichello	2
Pedro Diniz	1
Johnny Herbert	1

CONSTRUCTORS' CHAMPIONSHIP

McLaren-Mercedes	75
Ferrari	39
Benetton-Playlife	16
Williams-Mecachrome	16
Arrows	4
Sauber-Petronas	4
Stewart-Ford	2

grand prix player's du
canada

as the mclarens come over all fragile, a man who is anything but (he has a red car and a german passport) reveals every side of his complex character – and wins

Scot free: David Coulthard was so fast at the second start that his McLaren would have been on about page 65 when this was taken (left). Behind him, the (generally) more sensible of the Schumachers shows his ambitious sibling the correct way around the first turn as Frentzen, Alesi and Hill lead those who are about to pile into each other. Again. The crowd was already used to this sort of thing (above).

The 1998 Canadian Grand Prix was a race with everything. Pace, passion, drama, danger, heart-in-the-mouth skill, blood-curdling stupidity – and a deserving winner who somehow contrived to be a sore loser.

All of the above could apply to one man: Michael Schumacher. The Ferrari ace's demolition of a field which, to be fair, did a pretty good job of demolishing itself under-lined his status as the crown prince of the current F1 generation. But it also raised the same old questions about how far the German would go to win – the sort of stuff we all heard after Adelaide 1994 and Jerez 1997.

For this triumph Schumacher really had to dig deep, and perhaps the pressure told. He made a brilliant start, only for it to be negated by a potentially horrendous first-corner

blasts from the past

MICHAEL Schumacher blasts Damon Hill. Damon Hill slams Michael Schumacher. It all had a familiar ring to it – even if it was the best part of three years since the old enemies had crossed swords on track. When they did so again in Canada, sparks flew.

What appeared an innocuous incident to the untrained eye – Hill weaving in front of Schumacher on the approach to the final chicane as he tried to defend second place – escalated into a spectacular spat.

"If someone wants to kill you, he should do it in a different way," Schumacher told the world on live TV. "We were doing 200 mph down there and to move off line three times was simply unacceptable. It is impossible for such an experienced man to do this. I can't handle it and will have words with him."

Hill was armed with plenty of choice phrases of his own, however: "He's obviously got a massive problem," he said. "He can't claim anyone drives

accident in which Alexander Wurz's Benetton barrel-rolled and sucked in a third of the field. But the German's getaway at the restart was lousy and he was forced to spend the first quarter of the race examining the rear wing of fastest qualifier David Coulthard.

Yet McLaren helped make things easier. Points leader Mika Hakkinen had retired with a broken gearbox at the start and then

it raised the same old questions about how far the German would go to win – the sort of stuff we all heard after Adelaide 1994 and Jerez 1997

Fizzychella: Benetton's young gun (right) might well have been popping the cork to celebrate his first F1 victory. . . but for a gearbox malfunction and the not inconsiderable tenacity of Mr M Schumacher.

No parking: "I'm sorry Mr Trulli, you have just failed your driving test. There was a slight hitch when you tried to reverse around the first corner." Alesi was the man with the first-class view of a Prost undertray at the second start (far left).

young and bold

WHEN Benetton took the bold decision to pair fresh-faced twentysomethings Giancarlo Fisichella and Alexander Wurz in the F1 equivalent of a YTS scheme, paddock pundits were prepared to stake bets that they would end the year with more damaged cars than points.

They left Montreal with both, although there were few complaints from the Enstone team.

"The atmosphere here is simply marvellous," gushed boss David Richards afterwards. "It's driving everybody along."

Perhaps, marvellous wasn't the word for the atmosphere off or on the track after the first start. Wurz, scything down the inside at the first corner, played a central part in a multi-car accident which sent him barrel-rolling over Jean Alesi and Jarno Trulli. The common consensus was that he betrayed his lack of experience by applying the anchors too late.

"I could have braked on the start line and I wouldn't have been there, but we are meant to be racing," responded the Austrian. "There was just too little space for so many cars to get round the corner at once."

He betrayed no post-shunt nerves either – all the more commendable given that he'd just walked away from a brain-rattling crash in the tunnel at Monaco. After a quick trip to the loo he was out in the spare for Take Two – when Trulli was launched onto the back of Alesi's Sauber over the Benetton's front wheel.

"I didn't know where to go," Wurz explained. "It was a million per cent not my fault."

After all that, he raced strongly through the field in tandem with Irvine to collect a hitherto unlikely helping of points, while further up the road his transmission-troubled team-mate Fisichella was scoring better still despite being fleeced by Schumacher.

Not that Giancarlo saw it that way. "I think I did a good job, because on the shift up the gearbox was sometimes there, sometimes not," he said. "It was very difficult to be consistent."

But with two podiums in as many races, he and his team were making a difficult job look easy – although it wouldn't be long before the reverse was true.

badly when you look at the things he's been up to. He took Frentzen off the track completely. He knew he was there. I don't think you can give credibility to much of what Michael has to say."

Schumacher thought he had enough evidence to merit a stewards' ruling, though none arrived. Not that the laid-back Hill was particularly bothered – which was surprising, given that engine trouble had forced him to retire when a podium finish was a real possibility.

"Michael always seems to be angry with me about something," he shrugged. "We were racing for second: I'm not going to give it to him. I made it hard to pass and he still got through a very narrow gap.

"I'm surprised he did, but that's what he's good at. He's got nothing to complain about: instead of bitching, he should be happy he won the race and forget about it."

Roll model: Wurz recovered from his initial blunder (above left) to take fourth place in the spare Benetton.

Mouldy old foes: Michael and Damon still don't send each other birthday cards, apparently (far left).

the incident
with Frentzen
left a stain on
Schumacher's
afternoon. A
post-race
slanging match
with Damon was
mouldy icing on
the cake

Jacques attack: Villeneuve impressed his home audience with his car control (above), though he didn't have enough in reserve to sort out his ill-fated attempt to grab the lead.

throttle problems put paid to Coulthard on the 19th lap. After that Schumacher was out on his own – and it was here that he hit trouble.

Exiting the pits after his first stop Schumacher apparently failed to notice fourth-placed Heinz-Harald Frentzen screaming down his inside. He drove straight across the track, forcing the Williams onto the grass and into a pirouette which spelled retirement. Meanwhile, Michael made good his escape – but not for long.

"When I came out of the pits I was looking at the right side of the track," he said. "But you can only see at a certain angle, and his car must have been at that angle."

It sounded neither apologetic nor convincing. At least that's what the stewards thought, because they gave Schumacher a 10-second stop-go penalty which breathed new life into the race.

His punishment left three drivers with a good chance of victory – although Jacques Villeneuve wasted his by forgetting to engage his brain when he charged down the outside of Giancarlo Fisichella's Benetton to take the lead at Turn One. For a few metres, that is, before his Williams slithered through a gravel trap and out of contention.

That left Fisichella in the driving seat, though he was lapping increasingly erratically thanks to a dodgy gearbox.

Contender number three was Schumacher – and he didn't exactly need telling that there was still a whiff of victory in the air.

Twenty-two seconds behind the Benetton with 30 laps to go, he had breached the Roman's defence within 11 of them. Pure genius.

Yet the incident with Frentzen left a stain on Schumacher's afternoon. An ugly post-race slanging match with old foe Damon Hill was simply mouldy icing on the cake – and to complete the picture Williams protested his driving in vain.

But at least it hadn't been a dull afternoon in downtown Montreal.

7 Coulthard 1m 18.213s

8 Hakkinen 1m 18.282s

3 M Schumacher 1m 18.497s

5 Fisichella 1m 18.826s

10 R Schumacher 1m 19.242s

1 Villeneuve 1m 19.588s

2 Frentzen 1m 19.614s

4 Irvine 1m 19.616s

14 Alesi 1m 19.693s

9 Hill 1m 19.717s

6 Wurz 1m 19.765s

15 Herbert 1m 19.845s

18 Barrichello 1m 19.953s

12 Trulli 1m 20.188s

11 Panis 1m 20.303s

21 Takagi 1m 20.328s

17 Salo 1m 20.536s

22 Nakano 1m 21.230s

16 Diniz 1m 21.301s

19 Magnussen 1m 21.629s

23 Tuero 1m 21.822s

20 Rosset 1m 21.824s

FORMULA 1 WORLD CHAMPIONSHIP

7 June 1998 Circuit Gilles Villeneuve, Ile Notre Dame, Montreal
Circuit length: 2.747miles/4.421km

Pits Hairpin

Island Hairpin

Casino Corner

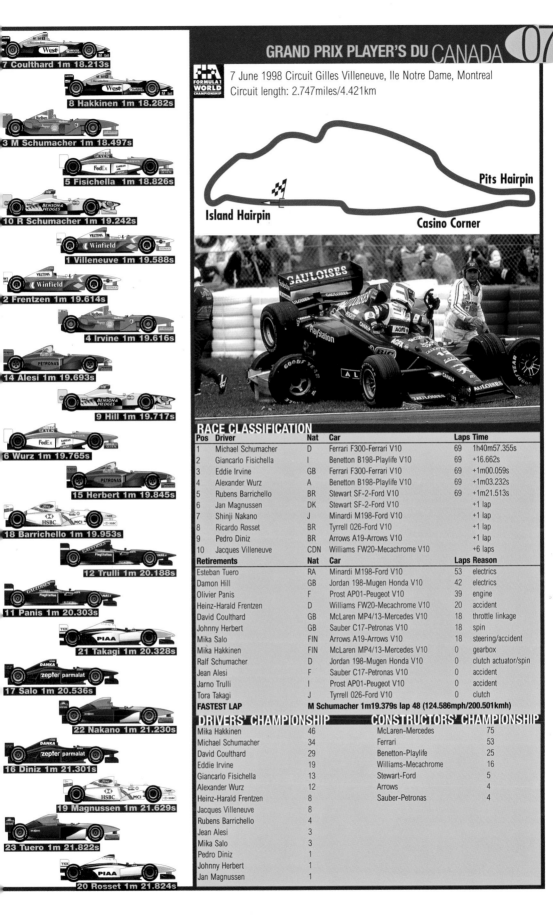

RACE CLASSIFICATION

Pos	Driver	Nat	Car	Laps	Time
1	Michael Schumacher	D	Ferrari F300-Ferrari V10	69	1h40m57.355s
2	Giancarlo Fisichella	I	Benetton B198-Playlife V10	69	+16.662s
3	Eddie Irvine	GB	Ferrari F300-Ferrari V10	69	+1m00.059s
4	Alexander Wurz	A	Benetton B198-Playlife V10	69	+1m03.232s
5	Rubens Barrichello	BR	Stewart SF-2-Ford V10	69	+1m21.513s
6	Jan Magnussen	DK	Stewart SF-2-Ford V10		+1 lap
7	Shinji Nakano	J	Minardi M198-Ford V10		+1 lap
8	Ricardo Rosset	BR	Tyrrell 026-Ford V10		+1 lap
9	Pedro Diniz	BR	Arrows A19-Arrows V10		+1 lap
10	Jacques Villeneuve	CDN	Williams FW20-Mecachrome V10		+6 laps

Retirements	Nat	Car	Laps	Reason
Esteban Tuero	RA	Minardi M198-Ford V10	53	electrics
Damon Hill	GB	Jordan 198-Mugen Honda V10	42	electrics
Olivier Panis	F	Prost AP01-Peugeot V10	39	engine
Heinz-Harald Frentzen	D	Williams FW20-Mecachrome V10	20	accident
David Coulthard	GB	McLaren MP4/13-Mercedes V10	18	throttle linkage
Johnny Herbert	GB	Sauber C17-Petronas V10	18	spin
Mika Salo	FIN	Arrows A19-Arrows V10	18	steering/accident
Mika Hakkinen	FIN	McLaren MP4/13-Mercedes V10	0	gearbox
Ralf Schumacher	D	Jordan 198-Mugen Honda V10	0	clutch actuator/spin
Jean Alesi	F	Sauber C17-Petronas V10	0	accident
Jarno Trulli	I	Prost AP01-Peugeot V10	0	accident
Tora Takagi	J	Tyrrell 026-Ford V10	0	clutch

FASTEST LAP M Schumacher 1m19.379s lap 48 (124.586mph/200.501kmh)

DRIVERS' CHAMPIONSHIP

Mika Hakkinen	46
Michael Schumacher	34
David Coulthard	29
Eddie Irvine	19
Giancarlo Fisichella	13
Alexander Wurz	12
Heinz-Harald Frentzen	8
Jacques Villeneuve	8
Rubens Barrichello	4
Jean Alesi	3
Mika Salo	3
Pedro Diniz	1
Johnny Herbert	1
Jan Magnussen	1

CONSTRUCTORS' CHAMPIONSHIP

McLaren-Mercedes	75
Ferrari	53
Benetton-Playlife	25
Williams-Mecachrome	16
Stewart-Ford	5
Arrows	4
Sauber-Petronas	4

Herr tonic: Lots of men behind a wall squash together to see Michael Schumacher take another comfortable grand prix win (left). The German celebrated with team-mate Irvine (below). . . and then spoiled things by asking if this was Ferrari's first ever F1 one-two. History never was his strong point.

false start furore gives schuey a second chance and he makes the most of it as he races away to head ferrari's first one-two since spain 1990

grand prix de **france**

The French Grand Prix: halfway point in the championship season and the ideal time to reflect upon the previous four months. Unless, of course, you happened to be a member of the McLaren-Mercedes team.

Melbourne in March seemed a long, long time ago come Magny-Cours in June. In another hemisphere McLaren had looked a league apart from its rivals, but by France the cracks were

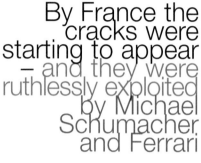

By France the cracks were starting to appear – and they were ruthlessly exploited by Michael Schumacher and Ferrari

starting to appear – and they were ruthlessly exploited by Michael Schumacher and Ferrari.

If you'd stuck a damp finger in the air, you could have been forgiven for thinking that the wind which had previously blown in the face of the Prancing Horse's title challenge was changing. Sure, Hakkinen qualified on pole – just – but Schumacher was right behind him, boosted by a development Goodyear tyre and tasty new aero bits on his F300. And Coulthard, used to acting as Hakkinen's rear watch if he wasn't on pole himself, was outgunned, pure and simple.

On Sunday Schumacher made the most of his new kit, even if – as on so many previous occasions – he needed luck to do it. This

french disconnection

came in the shape of an aborted first start after F1 returnee Jos Verstappen committed an error of the sort you are more likely to see courtesy of a septuagenarian Triumph Acclaim driver in the car park at Sainsbury's. He stalled his Stewart and the red lights came on as the field streaked away.

Hakkinen had made an inch-perfect getaway but it served little purpose as everyone was called back to try again.

Second time round it was Schuey who got the flyer – and that was the last the rest saw of him. Ferrari team-mate Irvine nipped ahead of both McLarens and stayed there, allowing Michael to stretch away to an easy victory.

The Ulsterman compounded Ferrari's joy

Cash helmet: Olivier Panis's lid (above) bears allegiance to French TV giant Canal + – and guess what most of France was watching at World Cup time, rather than their home grand prix?

Loyal supporter: Irvine played his role of understudy almost to perfection by holding off the McLarens (far left). True, Coulthard did pass him briefly... but within minutes the Scot was undone by a faulty refuelling rig. Hakkinen (pictured), however, could not unseat the Ulsterman.

Specs appeal: The immediate future actually wasn't so bright, but Coulthard and Hakkinen both felt compelled to wear shades (left).

MAGNY-COURS is the place F1 people love to hate – for several reasons. It is located in the middle of nowhere, it is nearly always ridiculously hot and stuffy – and the air is dense with a particularly vicious breed of mosquito.

Not that they had much going for them *à la carte* this time around as the paddock and grandstands were more deserted than usual.

World Cup fever had gripped the country – and how. Everywhere you went there were groups of mechanics, engineers, team bosses and even drivers clustered around TV sets in garage corners. Sudden, mysterious cheering disrupted tedious press conferences. And when England played Colombia on Friday evening, the business of motor racing went out of the window completely in an orgy of nationalistic fervour.

For now it was all very bright if you were English – David Beckham wasn't due to kick anyone until the following Wednesday – but no one was sufficiently distracted to believe the quoted attendance figures. The organiser claimed 75,000 but that was scarcely credible if you cast an eye over the vast prairie of empty plastic seats – and there were also rumours that a pile of tickets had been given away to local schools in a bid to boost the body count.

The secondary problem was that the track action on Sunday rated no better for entertainment value than a 0-0 draw between the United Arab Emirates and Faroe Islands reserves, despite Mika Hakkinen's best efforts to liven it up.

Some blamed the new technical rules – grooved tyres and narrower cars – for reducing the window of opportunity for passing; others said that aerodynamics, in particularly massive levels of downforce, had developed so far that F1 was disappearing up its own high-tech backside.

Even so, when the World Cup wasn't on it was no problem putting backsides on seats at races. It was just a shame that, like the football, the action so often failed to live up to the hype.

69

oranges are not the only fruit

by completing its first 1-2 in eight years – a process aided when the Silver Arrows self-destructed. First Hakkinen spun while trying to pass the unhelpful Irvine, then Coulthard – who breezed past Fast Eddie moments after his team-mate's bungle – lost a stack of time in the pits. The McLaren refuelling hose was in square peg/round hole mode when DC pulled in – and that forced him to making a flurry of pit stops which left him in contention for nothing more than a solitary point. That was a shame for the Scot because the recovered Hakkinen never did find a way by Irvine, despite a desperate sideways lunge at the very last corner.

The rest, from fourth-placed Jacques Villeneuve down, were bit players on a stuffy afternoon when staying power seemed to matter as much as skill. Which was interesting, because it was the first time that McLaren's had really been called into question.

MOST grand prix drivers tend to bring the same sort of baggage to races: private jet, chunky wrist-watch, statuesque model girlfriend hanging from the arm.

But not Jos Verstappen.

The Dutchman signalled his return to Formula One by bringing a more down-to-earth toy to Magny-Cours: a fruit cannon capable of splattering hapless oranges against unsuspecting targets with such force that it alarmed his new team Stewart as much as it amused them.

This form of recreation is typical of the uncomplicated Verstappen. Without a drive when Tyrrell's new owner opted for Ricardo Rosset's dollars rather than Jos's proven speed, he was left kicking his heels on the sidelines for six months. Rather than hang around the paddock like a spare part, however, Jos chose to bide his time at home playing with his young son and tinkering with kart engines, confident that he'd get another opportunity in the big time.

Thou shalt not pass: Wurz heads the pack as Alesi, Fisichella and Trulli get a reminder that the only overtaking you do at Magny-Cours is on the N7, the road which leads from the town of Nevers to the track. And the N7 isn't particularly thrilling, either.

Verstappen clearly wasn't entirely comfortable with the fact that his chance should come at the expense of Jan Magnussen, who had been given the red card by Stewart despite scoring his maiden point in Canada. Even so, the Dutchman accepted that time had been running short.

"I had offers to do other things, but I wasn't sure it was a good idea," he said. "In F1, it doesn't take long for your name to be forgotten."

That said, it was unlikely that either Mika Hakkinen or McLaren-Mercedes would forget him in a hurry, after Verstappen's stalled Stewart caused the first start to be aborted and provided the platform for Schumacher to humble everybody else. Despite this blunder Jos recovered to follow team-mate Barrichello home, having qualified encouragingly close to the Brazilian.

"The best is yet to come," he predicted. "I'm reasonably happy with how we got on here, but I know I can get more out of the car."

His manager, ex-GP driver Huub Rothengatter, was complaining about a lack of the right kind of Dutch oranges with which to arm the fruit cannon. But the signs were that his driver had more than enough firepower in his own armoury.

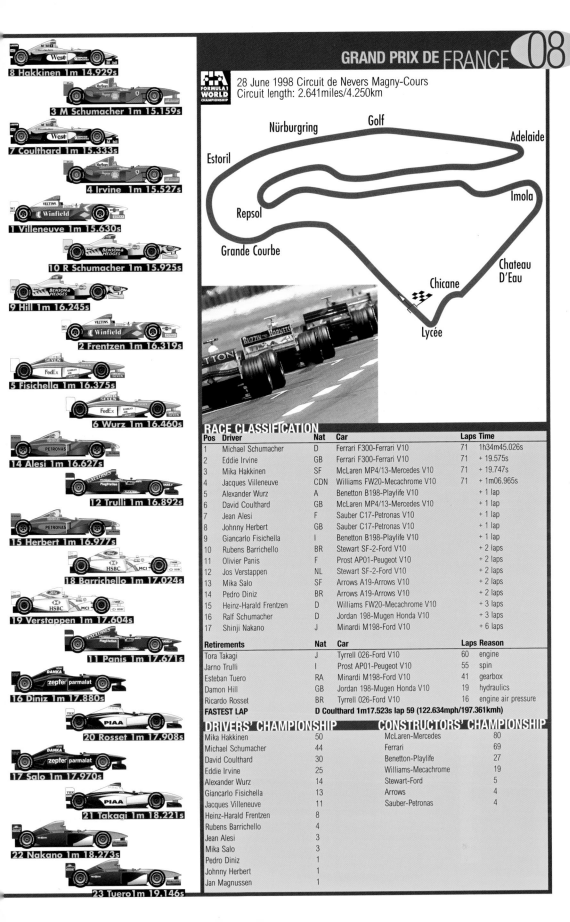

Starting Grid

8 Hakkinen 1m 14.929s
3 M Schumacher 1m 15.159s
7 Coulthard 1m 15.333s
4 Irvine 1m 15.527s
1 Villeneuve 1m 15.630s
10 R Schumacher 1m 15.925s
9 Hill 1m 16.245s
2 Frentzen 1m 16.319s
5 Fisichella 1m 16.375s
6 Wurz 1m 16.460s
14 Alesi 1m 16.627s
12 Trulli 1m 16.892s
15 Herbert 1m 16.977s
18 Barrichello 1m 17.024s
19 Verstappen 1m 17.604s
11 Panis 1m 17.671s
16 Diniz 1m 17.880s
20 Rosset 1m 17.908s
17 Salo 1m 17.970s
21 Takagi 1m 18.221s
22 Nakano 1m 18.273s
23 Tuero 1m 19.146s

FIA FORMULA 1 WORLD CHAMPIONSHIP

28 June 1998 Circuit de Nevers Magny-Cours
Circuit length: 2.641miles/4.250km

Nürburgring
Golf
Adelaide
Estoril
Imola
Repsol
Grande Courbe
Chateau D'Eau
Chicane
Lycée

RACE CLASSIFICATION

Pos	Driver	Nat	Car	Laps	Time
1	Michael Schumacher	D	Ferrari F300-Ferrari V10	71	1h34m45.026s
2	Eddie Irvine	GB	Ferrari F300-Ferrari V10	71	+ 19.575s
3	Mika Hakkinen	SF	McLaren MP4/13-Mercedes V10	71	+ 19.747s
4	Jacques Villeneuve	CDN	Williams FW20-Mecachrome V10	71	+ 1m06.965s
5	Alexander Wurz	A	Benetton B198-Playlife V10		+ 1 lap
6	David Coulthard	GB	McLaren MP4/13-Mercedes V10		+ 1 lap
7	Jean Alesi	F	Sauber C17-Petronas V10		+ 1 lap
8	Johnny Herbert	GB	Sauber C17-Petronas V10		+ 1 lap
9	Giancarlo Fisichella	I	Benetton B198-Playlife V10		+ 1 lap
10	Rubens Barrichello	BR	Stewart SF-2-Ford V10		+ 2 laps
11	Olivier Panis	F	Prost AP01-Peugeot V10		+ 2 laps
12	Jos Verstappen	NL	Stewart SF-2-Ford V10		+ 2 laps
13	Mika Salo	SF	Arrows A19-Arrows V10		+ 2 laps
14	Pedro Diniz	BR	Arrows A19-Arrows V10		+ 2 laps
15	Heinz-Harald Frentzen	D	Williams FW20-Mecachrome V10		+ 3 laps
16	Ralf Schumacher	D	Jordan 198-Mugen Honda V10		+ 3 laps
17	Shinji Nakano	J	Minardi M198-Ford V10		+ 6 laps

Retirements	Nat	Car	Laps	Reason
Tora Takagi	J	Tyrrell 026-Ford V10	60	engine
Jarno Trulli	I	Prost AP01-Peugeot V10	55	spin
Esteban Tuero	RA	Minardi M198-Ford V10	41	gearbox
Damon Hill	GB	Jordan 198-Mugen Honda V10	19	hydraulics
Ricardo Rosset	BR	Tyrrell 026-Ford V10	16	engine air pressure

FASTEST LAP D Coulthard 1m17.523s lap 59 (122.634mph/197.361kmh)

DRIVERS' CHAMPIONSHIP

Mika Hakkinen	50
Michael Schumacher	44
David Coulthard	30
Eddie Irvine	25
Alexander Wurz	14
Giancarlo Fisichella	13
Jacques Villeneuve	11
Heinz-Harald Frentzen	8
Rubens Barrichello	4
Jean Alesi	3
Mika Salo	3
Pedro Diniz	1
Johnny Herbert	1
Jan Magnussen	1

CONSTRUCTORS' CHAMPIONSHIP

McLaren-Mercedes	80
Ferrari	69
Benetton-Playlife	27
Williams-Mecachrome	19
Stewart-Ford	5
Arrows	4
Sauber-Petronas	4

i am the
passenger

...so sang iggy pop
back in 1977. but
when the voice of f1
hitched a lift with
mclaren, the only
thing singing was
a mercedes v10.
murray walker just
sat in awe

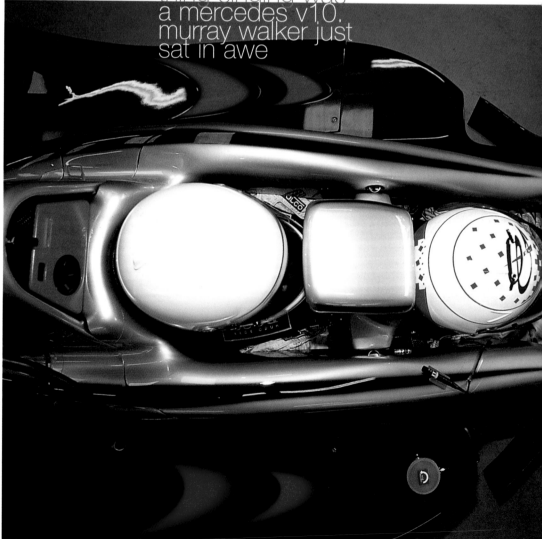

The average bloke who gets out of a modern F1 car is in his twenties (just about, in some cases) and implausibly fit. But Murray Walker, spearhead of ITV's F1 commentary team, is not exactly what you'd call average. Celebrating his 75th summer this year, he has been glued to a radio or television microphone for twice as long as many of his modern-day subjects have been on the planet. Yet when McLaren unveiled its revolutionary two seater F1 car in Melbourne, Walker's first reaction was to wonder how he could cadge a lift.

"As soon as they announced the car, I thought, 'My god I'd like a ride in that', though I didn't know how the hell you would go about it," he says. "It was fairly obvious that everybody would be applying to have a go, but fortunately for me ITV wanted to do a feature and I think [McLaren boss] Ron Dennis was aware of the publicity benefits."

But before anyone climbed into the two-seater, there was a stiff medical examination to be passed. For Murray, a regular health club visitor, this held no fears.

Indeed, he did rather better than certain of his substantially younger media colleagues.

Did you ever have any fears that the medical might stop you having a go?

"Not really. I knew what I was in for and I had to do a two-hour test at a big heart hospital in London. It was pretty stringent with a discussion about health in general, a spine X-ray, chest X-ray and treadmill tests. Fortunately I do a much tougher treadmill regime twice a week in my local health club than the one they put me through, and so I passed.

"I would have been very disappointed if I hadn't, but there was one thing worrying me slightly from a physical point of view. Having had both hips replaced, I thought something strange might happen to them at 3g in the middle of a corner, like popping out of their sockets. I could vaguely imagine them lifting me out of the car with my legs dangling all over the place."

Two's company: Martin Brundle and Murray Walker are accustomed to sharing a confined space at Silverstone (far left)... but there is usually some room for a cup of coffee and the odd TV monitor.

Murray minced: The chauffeur informs his passenger that, as a matter of fact, he has never, ever driven an F1 car on the latest grooved tyres before (above).

Did you get a perverse sense of pride that certain of your media colleagues (all right, it was Stan Piecha from *The Sun*) had failed?

"Oh yes. When I heard that Stan had gone down in flames I thought it was terrific."

Were you apprehensive at all about getting in the car?

"No. I had to go down to Woking to have a seat fitting and during that I talked a lot to [designer] Gordon Murray. He told me about the fond illusion they had at first, a belief that they could in some way modify the standard car. The more they went into it, however, the more they realised they had to build a new one, all the way down to building a new gearbox. My attitude was that McLaren had built it, so there was no doubting its integrity, and Martin Brundle was driving it. He's fast and safe and I knew he wouldn't be trying too hard to impress me, because I would be impressed if he only drove at 50 per cent of his capability. Honestly, I had no worries at all."

Vrooom without a view: The truth dawns on Murray that the commentary booth panorama isn't actually all that bad.

Sign of the times: Always popular with the fans, Murray gets a Boyzone-type reception for having shown that he could stick in Martin Brundle's slipstream for a handful of laps (below).

What's it like in there?

"The first thing is that when you get in you are totally immovable. Your legs are trapped between the inside of the tub and the outside of the driver's seat and there's a six-point harness which is completely tight. You have this great carbon fibre bar which literally traps you, because it's the support for the driver's seat and it's held in by four self-locking pins. You have the choice of putting your hands on your knees or across your chest but whichever you do you are quite trapped. I asked Martin what happens if we go off backwards into the bank and the bloody thing bursts into flames, and he said, 'Oh it wouldn't do that because there's hardly any petrol in it'."

What's the first sensation you remember as you took off?

"I was enormously impressed by the acceleration and the noise – even when we were still coming out of the pit lane. We all know what they sound like outside but when you are only a few inches in front of the engine. . . it's hard to describe."

How much time did you get in the car? It wasn't exactly a grand prix distance, was it?

"McLaren dictated that no one should do more than three laps, because of the neck loads, and at my medical they recommended

It wasn't so much the speed which impressed, it was the gigantic loads – the acceleration, deceleration and g forces

that I wear a support because the discs are very thin at my age. Anyway, nobody has done more than three laps – except me. We did three in the wet in the morning but Martin didn't think it was very impressive and he wanted to give me a run in the dry, to see what it was really like. It did dry out and over the lunch hour he asked me if I thought I could stand five laps, which would give him chance to get warmed up and do a couple of quick ones. I decided I'd stand five laps even if it killed me, because it was going to be the one and only opportunity I had to do this.

"They showed me the telemetry afterwards and we were touching 190mph down to Stowe, pulling 3g through some of the corners, so Martin gave me a really good idea of how it feels. It wasn't so much the speed which impressed, it was the gigantic loads – the acceleration, deceleration, g forces. . . and sometimes it felt like I was subjected to all of them at the same time. You just feel totally assaulted."

Have you ever done anything with even remotely comparable sensations?

"No, apart from driving a McLaren myself many years ago – but that was pathetically incompetent!"

What could you see from behind Brundle?

"Out of the appropriate eye you can see either right or left wheel and suspension and the track rushing past. If you are determined enough and you cock your head to the side you get a view alongside the driver's helmet and you see quite a lot."

Was there a singular, most impressive element?

"The deceleration. Martin said to me beforehand that it was the first time he had driven on grooved tyres, so I thought 'Oh god. . .' He had also warned me, however, that at various points around the circuit I would think he had missed his braking point, but that he wouldn't have done. I was watching the apex getting closer and closer at Abbey as we came in at about 160 or whatever with no sign of reduced speed. I remember thinking, 'This is what he said it would be like so I suppose it's all right', and of course it was. But you don't half stop in a hurry."

Given that you already regard everyone from Esteban Tuero upwards as a kind of demi-god, has this raised your perceptions at all about what the drivers do?

"Absolutely. How the hell they cope in a race I don't know, particularly at somewhere like Monaco, what with the forces – plus the heat and the competition."

Would you do it again?

"This afternoon, if I got the chance – except that I've just had my lunch."

rac british grand prix

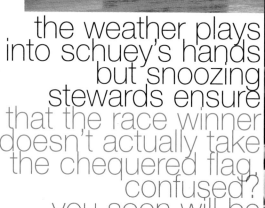

the weather plays into schuey's hands but snoozing stewards ensure that the race winner doesn't actually take the chequered flag, confused? you soon will be

Merc in the murk: Safety Car driver Oliver Gavin finished second in the supporting Porsche Supercup race and then had plenty of opportunity to prove that he could give Hakkinen and co a run for their money in his CLK (above). Ralf Schumacher congratulates his perplexed brother (right), though it's not clear whether Michael is stunned a) by what is going on or b) by the fact that his kid brother has actually finished a race.

Michael Schumacher is usually God's gift to TV cameras when he wins a race. Fists hammering the air, leaping all over the place, exultant back-slapping and hugging – this man can muster victory celebrations to put an entire World Cup-winning football squad in the shade.

For a few long minutes at Silverstone, though, it seemed as though the German had chucked away a winning lottery ticket. As he eased his way back to the pits after a controversial last-lap stop-go penalty, Schumacher showed no sign of glee after putting one over the McLarens in their backyard.

And that was because he wasn't entirely sure he had won. In fact, nobody could be completely sure until a couple of weeks later, when McLaren's protest against Ferrari's third victory of the season was thrown out of a Paris court.

By then, pretty much everybody outside of the Ferrari and McLaren camps had ceased caring. But the furore capped a British Grand

once the safety car had come and gone, however, mika was on borrowed time: his mp4-13 had taken a huge battering

unclear
penalty desicion

Prix weekend that was as stormy off the track as it was on it.

That suited Schumacher, who takes to damp tracks like an amphibian. It also clearly hurt McLaren, whose Bridgestone tyres didn't appear so handy as the rain got worse. And worse. And then worse yet.

Poleman Hakkinen led in drizzle from the off, smartly followed by team-mate David Coulthard, who took clear delight in dispossessing Schumacher of second at Becketts.

But when it really started to pour in earnest, the tables were turned. A miffed Coulthard spun off trying to hang on to Hakkinen. Eddie

Penalty, referee?: Schuey comes in at the end of the race and leaves the crowd to go home bewildered.

STEWARDS, remarked one wag, belong behind a bar. At Silverstone, they could have found plentiful employment serving light refreshment to the legion of McLaren team personnel who felt wronged by the race result.

The controversy which marred the end of the grand prix began on lap 43, when Schumacher lapped Alexander Wurz's Benetton under a stationary yellow flag at Stowe. The normal punishment in such circumstances is a 10-second stop-go penalty. Schumacher knew all about them, having served one a month earlier at the Canadian Grand Prix, which he still won. But this time the punishment only arrived when it was too late.

Ferrari was not informed of Schumacher's offence – and the stewards' decision to give him a penalty – until three laps from the end of the race. By then, according to F1 rules, 10 seconds could simply be added to his total race time. Somewhat confused, Ferrari did a belt and braces job by bringing in their regenmeister on the final lap, even though this meant he never took the flag. Officials eventually scrubbed the penalty because it was badly administered.

But that was only the start of it. McLaren was enraged, reasoning that if Schumacher had been given the penalty when he committed the offence, Hakkinen could well have won. The team immediately lodged a protest, knowing the chances of what it saw as justice were slim. The only result was that the race stewards resigned several weeks later.

As far as the Woking team was concerned, though, the whole thing smacked of conspiracy: it would be good for the image of the sport, went the argument, if Ferrari won the world title. McLaren boss Ron Dennis had said as much to the British press before the race. But motorsport president Max Mosley rubbished the suggestion afterwards.

"Anyone who looks at all the races will realise there is no conspiracy," he said.

The whole affair – a farce of Brian Rix proportions – diverted attention from a number of worthy causes. Water baby Jean Alesi drove brilliantly to hold fourth until his Sauber broke, though at least he had a boat to go back to watch France win the World Cup; Ralf Schumacher rose from last to sixth to break Jordan's 1998 duck; and Benetton young guns Alex Wurz and Giancarlo Fisichella were incredibly mature in conditions better suited to yachts.

scot on the rocks

Irvine scorched up the order, displacing Damon Hill and Jacques Villeneuve, to establish his Ferrari in third. And Schumacher homed in on Hakkinen, who pirouetted wildly through the gravel at Bridge but somehow kept his lead.

Once the Safety Car had come and gone, however, Mika was on borrowed time: his MP4-13 had taken a huge battering in the excursion. A lap later, Schumacher slipped by when Mika ran wide at Becketts and it was all over.

Until a few laps at the end, that is, when news of a possible penalty for the race-leading Ferrari broke. Problem was, the team wasn't informed in time, although it added to the confusion by bringing Schumacher into the pits on his very last lap, just in case.

This meant, of course, that the British Grand Prix winner never actually took the chequered flag. Then again, it was that sort of race.

Third dimension: Irvine heads for his first podium finish at a circuit where he has traditionally been lucky to last more than a couple of laps. The following Benettons are about to get their last helping of points for several weeks.

BRITAIN expected – but David Coulthard didn't deliver. Silverstone was a flashpoint in his title battle with Mika Hakkinen, the Scot knowing that failure to win would put the title effectively beyond his reach barring intervention from a tartan-clad deity.

Unfortunately, the only Act of God that arrived was the rainstorm which spun Coulthard into a watery retirement.

Yet it was a fate the outraged DC felt sure he could have avoided had he been in his team-mate's shoes. Indeed, he drove superbly early on to recover from the most disappointing qualifying session of his career, moving up from fourth to second and demoting Schumacher in the process.

But as the rain ploughed down, Coulthard was brought into the pits and given intermediate tyres, McLaren's long-range forecast suggesting the heavens were about to close. Yet by the time Hakkinen pulled in moments later, the team's resident Michael Fish had changed his mind and deemed full wet-weather rubber more appropriate

All this came two laps too late for Coulthard, who was already stomping back to the pits having pirouetted off trying to pass a Benetton at soaking Abbey. Such was his anger, he admitted, that he ignored the fans and marshals he habitually finds time for in his haste to give vent to uncharacteristic fury.

"I've got to understand why as a team we had two different tyre [strategies] on the cars," he fumed. "That's why I'm so angry.

"Everything seems to be working against us. I was on a tyre which was basically a slick in wet conditions. This is getting frustrating, because in all the races I'm there. I'm trying to make a battle of it and I just don't seem to be able to keep it together."

Mercedes boss Norbert Haug dismissed suggestions that Coulthard had been deliberately disadvantaged.

To rub salt into his wounds, Coulthard's mantle as top home driver was seized by Eddie Irvine, who made hay while the rain poured to join team-mate Schumacher on the podium. But the wet conditions definitely dampened down all the other home fires.

Damon Hill ran strongly for Jordan until being overtaken by Irvine – who cheekily labelled him "a sad old man" afterwards – but he posted the race's first retirement when he spun at Brooklands.

Ditto Johnny Herbert later on, but not before he incurred the wrath of Sauber sparring partner Jean Alesi for failing to move out of his way. Johnny blamed radio interference, Alesi just interference.

"Next year it is him or me," hissed Jean. Ultimately, the Frenchman got his wish.

8 Hakkinen 1m 23.271s

3 M Schumacher 1m 23.720s

1 Villeneuve 1m 24.102s

7 Coulthard 1m 24.310s

4 Irvine 1m 24.436s

2 Frentzen 1m 24.442s

9 Hill 1m 24.542s

14 Alesi 1m 25.081s

15 Herbert 1m 25.084s

5 Fisichella 1m 25.654s

6 Wurz 1m 25.760s

16 Diniz 1m 26.376s

17 Salo 1m 26.487s

12 Trulli 1m 26.808s

19 Verstappen 1m 26.948s

18 Barrichello 1m 26.990s

21 Takagi 1m 27.061s

23 Tuero 1m 28.051s

22 Nakano 1m 28.123s

20 Rosset 1m 28.608s

10 R Schumacher (1m 25.461s)

R Schumacher and O Panis started from the back row due to infringements which resulted in their times being disallowed.

11 Panis (1m 26.847s)

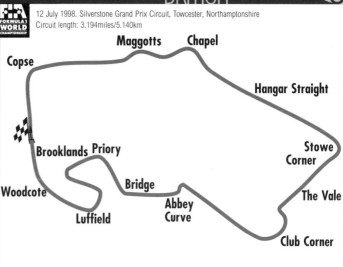

FIA FORMULA 1 WORLD CHAMPIONSHIP

12 July 1998. Silverstone Grand Prix Circuit, Towcester, Northamptonshire
Circuit length: 3.194miles/5.140km

Maggotts · Chapel · Copse · Hangar Straight · Stowe Corner · Brooklands · Priory · Woodcote · Bridge · Abbey Curve · Luffield · The Vale · Club Corner

RACE CLASSIFICATION

Pos	Driver	Nat	Car	Laps	Time
1	Michael Schumacher	D	Ferrari F300-Ferrari V10	60	1h47m12.450s
2	Mika Hakkinen	FIN	McLaren MP4/13-Mercedes V10	60	+12.465s
3	Eddie Irvine	GB	Ferrari F300-Ferrari V10	60	+19.199s
4	Alexander Wurz	A	Benetton B198-Playlife V10		+1 lap
5	Giancarlo Fisichella	I	Benetton B198-Playlife V10		+1 lap
6	Ralf Schumacher	D	Jordan 198-Mugen Honda V10		+1 lap
7	Jacques Villeneuve	CDN	Williams FW20-Mecachrome V10		+1 lap
8	Shinji Nakano	J	Minardi M198-Ford V10		+2 laps
9	Tora Takagi	J	Tyrrell 026-Ford V10		+4 laps

Retirements		Nat	Car	Laps	Reason
Jean Alesi		F	Sauber C17-Petronas V10	53	gearbox
Pedro Diniz		BR	Arrows A19-Arrows V10	45	spin
Olivier Panis		F	Prost AP01-Peugeot V10	40	spin
Rubens Barrichello		BR	Stewart SF-2-Ford V10	39	spin
Jos Verstappen		NL	Stewart SF-2-Ford V10	38	engine
David Coulthard		GB	McLaren MP4/13-Mercedes V10	37	spin
Jarno Trulli		I	Prost AP01-Peugeot V10	37	spin
Ricardo Rosset		BR	Tyrrell 026-Ford V10	29	spin
Esteban Tuero		RA	Minardi M198-Ford V10	29	spin
Johnny Herbert		GB	Sauber C17-Petronas V10	27	spin
Mika Salo		FIN	Arrows A19-Arrows V10	27	spin
Heinz-Harald Frentzen		D	Williams FW20-Mecachrome V10	15	spin
Damon Hill		GB	Jordan 198-Mugen Honda V10	13	spin

FASTEST LAP M Schumacher 1m35.704s lap 12 (120.140mph/193.346kmh)

DRIVERS' CHAMPIONSHIP

Mika Hakkinen	56
Michael Schumacher	54
David Coulthard	30
Eddie Irvine	29
Alexander Wurz	17
Giancarlo Fisichella	15
Jacques Villeneuve	11
Heinz-Harald Frentzen	8
Rubens Barrichello	4
Jean Alesi	3
Mika Salo	3
Pedro Diniz	1
Johnny Herbert	1
Jan Magnussen	1
Ralf Schumacher	1

CONSTRUCTORS' CHAMPIONSHIP

McLaren-Mercedes	86
Ferrari	83
Benetton-Playlife	32
Williams-Mecachrome	19
Stewart-Ford	5
Arrows	4
Sauber-Petronas	4
Jordan-Mugen Honda	1

the brit awards

for britain's four f1 drivers it was a season of sky-scraping highs and barrel-scraping lows. we look back on the home-spun quartet's full gamut of emotions, from damon hill's belgian grand prix victory to why the word "pliers" raises johnny herbert's hackles. . .

DAVID COULTHARD

1998 record. Races: 16. **Wins:** 1. **Poles:** 3. **Fastest laps:** 4. **Points:** 56. **Championship position:** 3rd

What went right? On his day, Coulthard looked every inch the world title contender his Williams years suggested he should be. He drove beautifully on occasion, won handsomely at Imola, watched at least two potential victories go up in smoke, handed another to team-mate Mika Hakkinen in Australia and generally looked more than a suitable foil for what was clearly the best car in the field. His efforts made sure of the constructors' crown so highly prized by his McLaren team, which was more than happy to renew his contract for 1999 – when he should get a second bite at the championship cherry.

What went wrong? Bluntly, he wasn't out there to win the constructors' crown, but to mount a convincing challenge for the drivers' title: something that just never happened, despite a promising start. David ran out of steam during a barren mid-season period which yielded just one point from four races: he was never the force he should have been thereafter, despite a string of podiums, and was badly overshadowed by Hakkinen in the final analysis. The situation did nothing to ease suspicions that the Finn is the team's favoured son, but on this showing he deserved to be.

Best race? His brilliant recovery from last to second at the Austrian Grand Prix.

Worst race? A toss-up between Silverstone and Spa.

Defining moment? The Italian Grand Prix. Coulthard takes the lead from the clearly slower Hakkinen and starts easing away before his engine goes bang. Cue a long walk back to the pits – and the chance to exchange a few choice words with partisan Ferrari fans.

Best-kept secret? Hot-footed it to the

McLaren factory the week after the British Grand Prix to apologise to team boss Ron Dennis in person, after a few choice words appeared in the papers suggesting Hakkinen had received preferential treatment on tyres.

How did he compare to his team-mate? Not well enough. Early on he and Hakkinen were beautifully matched, and after his victory at Imola you would have got good odds on DC matching Mika's title bid point for point. But the Italian race was a watershed: from Barcelona onwards the Finn seemed to snatch another gear and race away while Coulthard became mired in a run of misfortune. As the season wore on he had little choice but to assume the mantle of Hakkinen's rear gunner. It was a role he performed with distinction, but it wasn't what he had auditioned for.

Our verdict? It could all have been so different if he'd had mid-season reliability at races such as Monaco and Canada, which could have been the bedrock of a title challenge. But they weren't and so this was an opportunity missed rather than knocked.

DAMON HILL

1998 record. Races: 16. **Wins:** 1. **Poles:** 0. **Fastest laps:** 0. **Points:** 20. **Championship position:** 6th

What went right? A fairy tale win at Spa topped off a season which recovered, along with Hill's reputation, from early-season misery. Once Jordan got its car and engine sorted, the 38-year-old Englishman was always a contender, dragging his team into contention for third place in the constructors' championship and confounding any critics who dared still to claim that he owed his 1996 world title solely to Williams. On balance, this was a year when Hill showed some class and proved that Jordan paid him a reputed £5 million retainer for a lot more than pure PR value.

once jordan got its car and engine sorted, the 38-year-old englishman was always a contender

What went wrong? Just about everything until he broke his duck with fourth place at the German Grand Prix. If Jordan under-performed in the first half of the year, so did Hill, who looked neither motivated nor hungry. Struggled to hide his early disappointment and word leaked out of a helmet-throwing garage strop in Argentina, along with rumours that he would quit at the end of the season if situation didn't improve. Fortunately, it didn't come to that.

Best race? Belgium, as if you needed to ask. A richly deserved victory for both man and team.

Worst race? Monaco, where he was almost caught by Shinji Nakano's Minardi – having enjoyed a joke at the Italian team's expense during a pre-race press conference.

Defining moment? A year of such contrasting fortunes that it's hard to pick one out. For old times' sake, we'll say Canada – a feisty battle with Michael Schumacher followed by a post-race barney. It was like 1995 all over again. . .

Best-kept secret? A deflating tyre came within a lap of costing him his glorious Spa win. A well-timed pit stop saved the day.

How did he compare to his team-mate? Well enough to boost both their reputations. Ralf Schumacher was the one with the point to prove, which he did by out-qualifying Hill more often than not in the first half of the year and scoring points more regularly. But it was Damon who won in Spa – and he proved he could match Schu Jnr's blistering speed when it mattered.

Result? Jordan leapt up the points table, Ralf secured a Williams drive and Hill emerged with his reputation intact. Honours even, we'd say.

Our verdict? A silk purse from a sow's ear if ever there was one. Should be well-placed to challenge for more wins in 1999, although Jordan's all-round consistency needs to improve.

EDDIE IRVINE

1998 record. Races: 16. **Wins:** 0. **Poles:** 0 **Fastest laps:** 0. **Points:** 47. **Championship position:** 4th

What went right? This was the year when Irvine grew up, maturing into a solid race day performer with an uncanny knack of squeezing onto the podium no matter where he finished the first lap – see Canada for conclusive proof. Being Michael Schumacher's team-mate meant he seldom got the chance to do anything other than play second fiddle. But when that's good enough to net fourth in the world championship and a hatful of points, the "worst job in F1" suddenly doesn't look so bad.

What went wrong? Very little, apart from a couple of forgettable races and the fact that his situation at Ferrari meant he could never translate pushing for points and podiums into challenging for wins. Couldn't resist the temptation to get involved in the odd bout of argy-bargy: both physical (with Fisichella in Spain) and verbal (clumsy cod-psychological criticisms of McLaren in the wake of the latter's mid-season woes).

Best race? Even-stevens between his stay-out-of-trouble third place the British GP, his crowd-pleasing blast into second behind Schumacher at Monza and Suzuka.

Worst race? His failure to keep Hakkinen behind him for long enough at the Nürburgring – for which he endured a hail of rhetorical rotten fruit from both inside and outside Ferrari.

Defining moment? Austria. Irvine heads for a lonely third until Schumacher – delayed by his altercation with a gravel trap works his way onto his tail. The Ulsterman eagerly hands the place to his team-mate, then tells everybody he had "brake problems". With a knowing grin.

Best-kept secret? Back pain from an ill-fitting seat which sapped his stamina in races. Not even visits to orthopaedic experts could help.

How did he compare to his team-mate? Come on, it's Michael Schumacher! What do you

he couldn't resist the temptation to get involved in the odd bout of argy-bargy: both physical (with fisichella in spain) and verbal

expect? In the circumstances, Irvine did pretty well, generally qualifying only slightly adrift of his exalted partner and even heading him on the grid occasionally. But it was always going to be a losing battle on race days, when a) Schumacher is the best and b) Ferrari's pit stop strategy was always tailored exclusively to the German's needs. But in supporting

Schumacher's title bid to the hilt, he did exactly what he was paid to do.

Our verdict? His best season in F1 by far. Dependable, mature and usually as quick as anyone bar his team-mate, he backed Schumacher up efficiently and did his own reputation a power of good.

JOHNNY HERBERT

1998 record. Races: 16. **Wins:** 0 **Poles:** 0. **Fastest laps:** 0. **Points:** 1 **Championship position:** 15th=

What went right? Er. . . pass! Very, very little after the Australian Grand Prix – where he notched up fifth on the grid and scored a point.

What went wrong? After Australia, pretty much everything. Sauber turned political thanks to the arrival of the mercurial Jean Alesi, and Herbert never looked comfortable trying to play the same game. To make matters worse, Alesi swiftly got the upper hand in races and began bringing home points regularly, going on to give Sauber its first front row start and a podium at Spa. By then it was clear that Herbert's days with the team were numbered: he had the lion's share of bad luck, but he didn't help his cause by falling out with Alesi when he refused to let

him past at Silverstone.

Best race? Australia. Clearly faster than Jacques Villeneuve, but unable to overtake the Williams, Herbert's tigering drive was full of conviction and deserved more than a solitary point.

Worst race? He reckons it was Argentina, a catalogue of disasters which began when Alesi inadvertently ran him off the road on their first practice lap. But Herbert's luck was generally so miserable that you could substitute several others.

Defining moment? The Luxembourg Grand Prix – a race ruined by an errant pair of pliers which were left in the Sauber's cockpit by his crew and kept jamming underneath his pedals.

Best-kept secret? A passion for his new Nissan Skyline GT-R road car – which, unsurprisingly, threatened to outstrip his enthusiasm for driving the Sauber C17.

How did he compare to his team-mate? Not as well as his early season showings suggested he would. Blew Alesi away to start with, only for Jean to return the favour with interest, hog the points and the limelight with some excellent drives.

Our verdict? A dispiriting end to a three-year career with Sauber which had done much to raise Herbert's morale and stock in the paddock.

grosser preis von
österreich

mclaren scores another 1-2 — despite coulthard dropping briefly to the tail of the field in a race packed with incident

Going, going. . : Hakkinen was passed by Schumacher for all of a nanosecond (left), but as Michael shapes up to make his move the awful truth will soon dawn that he won't make the corner. Despite everything, the podium looked fairly familiar come four in the afternoon (above).

The end result told a familiar enough story – although McLaren's fifth win in 10 races was something of a relief on the back of three straight Ferrari victories.

Or, rather, three straight Michael Schumacher victories.

Mika Hakkinen and David Coulthard picked up their fourth 1-2 of the year at the A1-Ring, but this was hardly a breeze.

Sure, Hakkinen was led only twice all afternoon but he had not had an easy time of it. The Finn was usurped, briefly, by his team-mate after he peeled in to make his routine fuel stop, but that was no threat to his eventual supremacy.

Far more of a potential menace was Schumacher, who led for all of a nanosecond in the early stages of the race.

The German pounced shortly after the field had been unfettered by the Safety Car, which was pressed into service after accidents at both the first and second corners at the original start. As the pace picked up

Schumacher tried to run around the outside of Hakkinen at Turn Three but, although he drew ahead of the McLaren, he was so far off line he was almost in the adjacent cow field. Hakkinen quickly regained the initiative as Schumacher's enthusiasm momentarily dropped him to third behind Giancarlo Fisichella.

Hakkinen's hopes for a peaceful afternoon were abruptly shattered when Schuey came storming back, but such was the Ferrari team leader's urgency that he later made a more serious error at the final corner and went bounding through the gravel.

As bits of red carbon fibre were sprinkled liberally through the outfield, the crowd actually had to stop drinking for a second to let out a groan which drowned out the sound of the recovering Ferrari.

For Hakkinen, the pressure was off.

"If it wasn't already looking like Mika's title

as bits of red carbon fibre were sprinkled liberally through the outfield, the crowd actually had to stop drinking for a second

Scot free: Coulthard (above) charged through the field to finish second. . . and then calmly pointed out that it was all very normal, because he had the best car. Despite his honesty, the FIA allowed him to keep his racing licence.

hero and villain

NOT only can the rain be a great leveller in a race, it can also throw in a few added unexpected twists beforehand.

So wet was it at one o'clock on Saturday that not even the Tyrrells and Minardis came out for the usual three minutes of TV exposure. Conditions improved as the session wore on, but not by much. The sight of Michael Schumacher skirting a gravel trap was evidence that the good and the great were no better off than their alleged inferiors in the circumstances.

For a few delicious moments it appeared that rain-lover Jean Alesi was on course to give Sauber its first-ever F1 pole, though he was beaten in the final few seconds by Giancarlo Fisichella – which was a first for him.

The two embraced warmly after facing the media, though few believed they would stay ahead for long with Hakkinen and Schumacher lining up directly behind.

At Spa in 1995 title contenders Schumacher and Damon Hill had lined up 16th and eighth in similar conditions. . . yet had still come through to finish first and second.

On that occasion it took them 15 laps to reach the top two places. At the A1-Ring it took Hakkinen and Schumacher just two corners to do the same and restore the perceived status quo.

Worse was to come for Saturday's glory boys as Fisichella came out of the pits following his scheduled stop and immediately tried to pass Alesi for fourth at Turn Two.

The move was never on and the two skated to a halt, Alesi retiring in almost same patch of gravel as he had 12 months earlier when he tangled with Irvine.

Guilty as Fisichella was, Alesi kept his feelings in check.

"I am very sorry it ended like this," said Jean, "all the more so because I really like Giancarlo."

The lost boys: Drama at Turn Two (top left) as Coulthard finds himself pincered in the middle of lots of people who get paid zillions for their (occasional) ability to control F1 cars.

First past the Prost: Villeneuve and the recovering Schumacher seek a route around Jarno Trulli, who was unable to provide any clues that he had actually led this very race one year earlier (above left). In the background Herbert makes a brave effort to stay sufficiently close that he gets his picture in the book.

Pole-axed: After topping the charts on Saturday Fisichella (above) came to earth with a bump when he clobbered Alesi (right) in the race.

year, it certainly is now," admitted Coulthard. "He's having a great run."

He was talking after a particularly good effort of his own. Starting a worst-ever 14th in the wake of the chaos that was wet-weather qualifying, he began the race thinking that it would be a result to score some points. By the second turn even that looked beyond him as the Arrows twins combined to shove him off the road. As he rejoined he was hit by Mika Salo as the Finn attempted a spin-turn and that knocked off the McLaren's nose wing.

"I didn't know that until I got to the next corner," said Coulthard, "but I was amazed that nothing else had broken because it was a big bang."

As he trailed to the pits the Safety Car was already providing him with a damage limitation cushion and Coulthard re-entered the fray without losing a lap – albeit dead last. By mid-race, however, he was second.

The Scot is a man who is well aware of his own abilities – but he also had his feet on the

weathering the
storm

ground. As a flotilla of journalists besieged him with questions about his mighty comeback David took it all in his stride.

"I'd rather have been racing from the front at the start," he said, "but it was very satisfying to come through the field like that.

"What you have to remember," he added, "is that it's much easier to do that when you have a car advantage – and McLaren certainly had that today."

There was rather less straightforward honesty at Ferrari.

Schumacher did his usual thing and sliced back through the field to reach fourth place – after briefly being delayed by his feisty younger brother, who was on form again.

That left only team-mate Eddie Irvine between the title challenger and the McLarens – and it was no surprise that Irvine's lap times suddenly fell away by two seconds until his number one was through to third.

Paranoid about any possible FIA reaction to team orders (a thorny subject since McLaren's very public switcharound in Australia), an excuse about brake problems was quickly rustled up.

Strangely, when Schumacher mentioned this, everyone laughed.

At least the governing body was moved to clarify the issue: team orders were quite okay so long as they weren't prejudicial to the interests of the sport – just as we'd all thought in the first place, in fact.

THE Germans enjoy their F1 weekends. In homage to Michael Schumacher they turn up days in advance to pitch camp, unfurl banners and drink beer.

Nowadays they are spoilt for venues, with two races on their home territory plus easily accessible events in Hungary, Belgium and, of course, Austria.

The camping facilities at the foot of the Styrian hills are plentiful. . . but also vulnerable.

Conditions in the build-up to this year's race were appalling. On Thursday night a three-hour electric storm caused flooding only a few kilometres down the road. While unfortunate locals cleared out the muddied remains of their wrecked ground floors, the camp site revellers could be thankful that they had escaped the worst of it.

Used to such situations (albeit on a lesser scale), the Austrians quickly had fire services and drainage equipment on the camp sites and were packing swamped areas with sand and stones to render them just about passable.

Through it all the banquets and drinking continued. At eight the following morning many fans were still shambling across the road bouncing off circuit-bound traffic that was attempting to thread through the human chaos at walking speed.

There was more heavy rain to come, too, but nature's fit of pique and a few wet clothes did far less to perturb the fans than their hero's Ferrari running off the track during its early pursuit of Mika Hakkinen.

Schuey stopper: The heavy rain caused rivers to burst their banks in the Tyrol region – and floods of tears in the camp sites as the crowd favourite (above) failed to conquer the McLarens. Barrichello (left) ran as high as fourth for Stewart. . . but the car failed to last the distance.

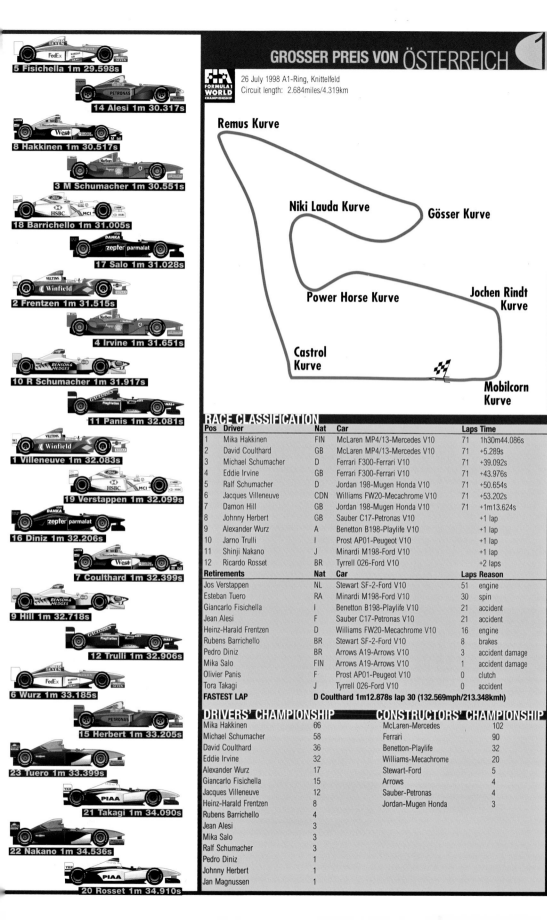

FIA FORMULA 1 WORLD CHAMPIONSHIP

26 July 1998 A1-Ring, Knittelfeld
Circuit length: 2.684miles/4.319km

Remus Kurve

Niki Lauda Kurve

Gösser Kurve

Power Horse Kurve

Jochen Rindt Kurve

Castrol Kurve

Mobilcorn Kurve

Qualifying times (left column):

- 5 Fisichella 1m 29.598s
- 14 Alesi 1m 30.317s
- 8 Hakkinen 1m 30.517s
- 3 M Schumacher 1m 30.551s
- 18 Barrichello 1m 31.005s
- 17 Salo 1m 31.028s
- 2 Frentzen 1m 31.515s
- 4 Irvine 1m 31.651s
- 10 R Schumacher 1m 31.917s
- 11 Panis 1m 32.081s
- 1 Villeneuve 1m 32.083s
- 19 Verstappen 1m 32.099s
- 16 Diniz 1m 32.206s
- 7 Coulthard 1m 32.399s
- 9 Hill 1m 32.718s
- 12 Trulli 1m 32.906s
- 6 Wurz 1m 33.185s
- 15 Herbert 1m 33.205s
- 23 Tuero 1m 33.399s
- 21 Takagi 1m 34.090s
- 22 Nakano 1m 34.536s
- 20 Rosset 1m 34.910s

RACE CLASSIFICATION

Pos	Driver	Nat	Car	Laps	Time
1	Mika Hakkinen	FIN	McLaren MP4/13-Mercedes V10	71	1h30m44.086s
2	David Coulthard	GB	McLaren MP4/13-Mercedes V10	71	+5.289s
3	Michael Schumacher	D	Ferrari F300-Ferrari V10	71	+39.092s
4	Eddie Irvine	GB	Ferrari F300-Ferrari V10	71	+43.976s
5	Ralf Schumacher	D	Jordan 198-Mugen Honda V10	71	+50.654s
6	Jacques Villeneuve	CDN	Williams FW20-Mecachrome V10	71	+53.202s
7	Damon Hill	GB	Jordan 198-Mugen Honda V10	71	+1m13.624s
8	Johnny Herbert	GB	Sauber C17-Petronas V10		+1 lap
9	Alexander Wurz	A	Benetton B198-Playlife V10		+1 lap
10	Jarno Trulli	I	Prost AP01-Peugeot V10		+1 lap
11	Shinji Nakano	J	Minardi M198-Ford V10		+1 lap
12	Ricardo Rosset	BR	Tyrrell 026-Ford V10		+2 laps

Retirements	Nat	Car	Laps	Reason
Jos Verstappen	NL	Stewart SF-2-Ford V10	51	engine
Esteban Tuero	RA	Minardi M198-Ford V10	30	spin
Giancarlo Fisichella	I	Benetton B198-Playlife V10	21	accident
Jean Alesi	F	Sauber C17-Petronas V10	21	accident
Heinz-Harald Frentzen	D	Williams FW20-Mecachrome V10	16	engine
Rubens Barrichello	BR	Stewart SF-2-Ford V10	8	brakes
Pedro Diniz	BR	Arrows A19-Arrows V10	3	accident damage
Mika Salo	FIN	Arrows A19-Arrows V10	1	accident damage
Olivier Panis	F	Prost AP01-Peugeot V10	0	clutch
Tora Takagi	J	Tyrrell 026-Ford V10	0	accident

FASTEST LAP D Coulthard 1m12.878s lap 30 (132.569mph/213.348kmh)

DRIVERS' CHAMPIONSHIP

Driver	Points
Mika Hakkinen	66
Michael Schumacher	58
David Coulthard	36
Eddie Irvine	32
Alexander Wurz	17
Giancarlo Fisichella	15
Jacques Villeneuve	12
Heinz-Harald Frentzen	8
Rubens Barrichello	4
Jean Alesi	3
Mika Salo	3
Ralf Schumacher	3
Pedro Diniz	1
Johnny Herbert	1
Jan Magnussen	1

CONSTRUCTORS' CHAMPIONSHIP

Constructor	Points
McLaren-Mercedes	102
Ferrari	90
Benetton-Playlife	32
Williams-Mecachrome	20
Stewart-Ford	5
Arrows	4
Sauber-Petronas	4
Jordan-Mugen Honda	3

grosser mobil 1 preis von
deutschland

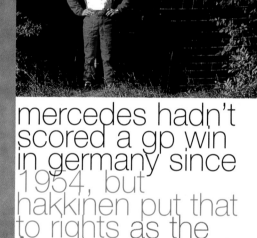

mercedes hadn't scored a gp win in germany since 1954, but hakkinen put that to rights as the ferraris struggled on schuey's home turf

Heir apparent beats Herr Apparent: Even though his McLaren sprang an oil leak, there was no stopping the victorious Hakkinen (left). There were fewer flares than usual in the packed Hockenheim stands as Mr Vexed of Kerpen (above) had to drive his nuts off for just a couple of points.

Here was manna for conspiracy theorists. In Austria, one week before the German Grand Prix, McLaren chief Ron Dennis had been to have a private word with Ferrari's Sporting Director Jean Todt.

Their meeting followed a series of open allegations by Dennis that there was something on the Ferrari F300 which did not comply with the F1 regulations and, lo and behold, the cars of Michael Schumacher and Eddie Irvine were way off the pace when they rolled out onto the characterless asphalt of Hockenheim.

Some felt it was tempting to believe that whatever Dennis has said had been enough to persuade Ferrari to change its car between races. Ferrari said that this was nonsense and that it wished Dennis would stop talking to the press and present whatever he was protesting to the FIA's technical commission at his

crash test dummies

Patrick Lemarié is not the most famous racing driver in the world. Chances are that he never will be. The Frenchman raced successfully up to F3 level in his homeland before trying his luck in North America.

When he came back he made it into Formula 3000 – supposedly no more than a knock on the door from Formula One – and then the money ran out.

Still, at least he had friends in high places – such as childhood pal Jacques Villeneuve and British American Racing prime mover Craig Pollock.

Hockenheim was supposed to be the prelude to Lemarié's big week. Once the race was over he was due to test a contemporary Tyrrell at Silverstone – but in Germany the team's current F1 line-up inadvertently made sure that, for now at least, F1 remained no more than a dream for Lemarié.

It started on Saturday morning when Ricardo Rosset (left) ran off the road and slammed into the tyre wall at Turn One. Familiar with not starting races because he hadn't driven fast enough, the Brazilian flew home early this time on medical advice. His car was junk and he was told to go away and take a rest. A plea from Tyrrell to let him race without taking part in official qualifying was turned down.

In qualifying his team-mate Tora Takagi completed a similar demolition job on one of the surviving Tyrrells at exactly the same point on

earliest convenience.

Given the hype it was an unfortunate time for the Prancing Horse to have an off-weekend, but if reason was applied then little else should have been expected. Recent history showed that Ferrari had been, frankly, rubbish at circuits where cars ran in low downforce trim. It was true at Hockenheim and Monza in 1997 and Schumacher was sure that it would be the same again

Catch the buzz: Damon Hill (right) finished fourth to score his first points for Jordan – and he was only a handful of seconds away from Hakkinen, too.

come on you yellows

No head for heights: Jacques Villeneuve tries to stop himself looking down (far left) after hauling his revitalised Williams into the top three. Remarkably, it was the reigning world champ's first podium finish of the season.

Let's wave even if they are cheering for the bloke who finished fifth: Hakkinen fails to score any extra points for holding Coulthard and Villeneuve off the ground in a clean straight lift (left). By 1998 standards, the sight of the French-Canadian on the podium was something rarer than an uncrashed Tyrrell.

the circuit.

Fortunately it is not too far to jog back to the pits and Takagi was soon strapped into the one surviving chassis.

Not 10 minutes after his accident, the TV slow-motion replay kicked in again to show Takagi going off at the first corner. It was assumed that this was just a replay of his earlier spectacular effort – until this time he veered away from the tyre wall at the last moment.

Unperturbed he lined up 15th and finished 13th. . . but such was the weekend's toll that the planned Silverstone test was pretty much like two of the team's cars.

Scrap.

At the start of the year Damon Hill was perceived as Jordan's missing link, the vital last ingredient needed to raise the team above its customary fifth place in the constructors' championship.

But after 10 races, we were still waiting to see the evidence.

At Hockenheim, finally, Hill managed to do what team-mate Ralf Schumacher had done in each of the previous two races and trouble the scorers.

It wasn't a solo effort. Ralf was fast again, too, but he undid himself with a two-stop strategy which allowed him to run third in the opening stages before he faded to sixth as those with a scrap of tactical nous opted for just one scheduled stop.

Step forward D Hill and virtually everyone else in the field.

Jordan had a new Mugen Honda V10 for qualifying (though it wasn't raced) and technocynics pointed to the fact that that the team traditionally goes well at circuits where a car's aerodynamic properties are less influential.

Initially fifth, Damon ran within sight of Jacques Villeneuve's much-improved Williams all afternoon before taking the flag just over seven seconds shy of winner Hakkinen – albeit in fourth place. (And there were times when he didn't get so close to Jacques when they both had a Williams.)

"The great thing was that we weren't just out there waiting for people to fall off," he said, "we were in a real competition and it was great to see the front of the field again. It was more like the sort of driving I have been used to, with people to chase and a bit of defending to do."

While Villeneuve kept a wary eye on Damon's progress, the Jordan star was aware that his closest challenger was his old nemesis Schumacher Snr.

In the end he managed to outrun him quite comfortably.

"I knew he was getting close at one point," he said, "but that in itself was great motivation."

He might not quite have got to drink the bubbly, but he certainly sounded it.

the crowd favourite didn't exactly help his own cause when he crashed on his first flying lap

Schuey polish: Ralf (above) was in the points for Jordan for the third successive race, though he might have done better than sixth but for a bonkers two-stop race strategy.

this time around.

The crowd favourite didn't exactly help his own cause when he crashed on his first flying lap on Saturday morning – an uncharacteristic error which amplified how much he was struggling – but there looked to be little chance of Ferrari threatening McLaren . . . unless they tripped one up while they were being lapped.

In the end it didn't quite come to that, but the Hockenheim auditorium was unusually subdued as Schumacher slaved to salvage a couple of points after starting ninth.

The McLarens led all the way, of course, and this time one had the feeling that David Coulthard was the faster of the two – though Mika Hakkinen picked up his sixth victory of the season.

"Even if I was a bit quicker," said Coulthard, "it's very hard to pass a car of equal performance and I wasn't about to take any silly risks. This was an important race for the championship and it was important for

Mercedes, too."

Indeed, Merc had not won its home race since 1954.

Coulthard felt his biggest chance was to overtake during the routine pit stops, but his in lap was stymied when he came across Takagi's Tyrrell and Salo's Arrows in the stadium. He rejoined the race half a second behind Hakkinen and stayed there to the end.

The world championship leader was giving McLaren some cause for concern, however. A computer readout suggested that the team might not have engaged enough fuel during the Finn's stop and so he was told to switch to a more economical management programme.

"The engine felt like it lost its edge a bit towards the end," said Mika, though Ron Dennis said this was consistent with what Mika had been told to do.

What the engine was losing, however, was oil. Coulthard was coated by the end of the race – and even the revitalised Jacques Villeneuve, charging along in third place and at one stage closing fast, got a faceful.

"I could see there was some sort of problem," said Villeneuve, "so it made sense to see if we could aggravate that."

In the end, however, the reigning world champion's Williams developed an electronic problem of its own and had to settle for what was – astonishingly – his first podium finish since he had clinched the title in Jerez the previous October.

For all that Coulthard's helmet, gloves and wing mirrors were coated in oil, however, McLaren insisted that there had been no problem. "There was nothing showing up on the telemetry," said Mercedes V10 designer Mario Illien, lighting up a cigar as the Rolling Stones began to blare out of the overworked CD player in the Mercedes motorhome, "so we were never worried. What covered David was simply excess oil blowing out of the breather tank."

Then he paused a moment.

"Or maybe," he said, "it was just champagne."

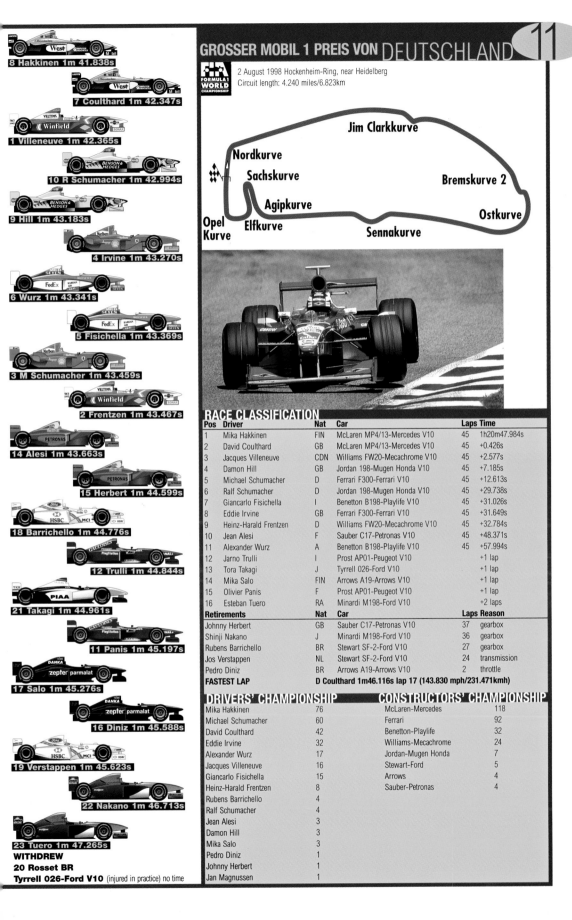

FIA FORMULA 1 WORLD CHAMPIONSHIP

2 August 1998 Hockenheim-Ring, near Heidelberg
Circuit length: 4.240 miles/6.823km

Jim Clarkkurve

Nordkurve

Sachskurve

Bremskurve 2

Agipkurve

Ostkurve

Opel Kurve

Elfkurve

Sennakurve

Qualifying times (left column):

- 8 Hakkinen 1m 41.838s
- 7 Coulthard 1m 42.347s
- 1 Villeneuve 1m 42.365s
- 10 R Schumacher 1m 42.994s
- 9 Hill 1m 43.183s
- 4 Irvine 1m 43.270s
- 6 Wurz 1m 43.341s
- 5 Fisichella 1m 43.369s
- 3 M Schumacher 1m 43.459s
- 2 Frentzen 1m 43.467s
- 14 Alesi 1m 43.663s
- 15 Herbert 1m 44.599s
- 18 Barrichello 1m 44.776s
- 12 Trulli 1m 44.844s
- 21 Takagi 1m 44.961s
- 11 Panis 1m 45.197s
- 17 Salo 1m 45.276s
- 16 Diniz 1m 45.588s
- 19 Verstappen 1m 45.623s
- 22 Nakano 1m 46.713s
- 23 Tuero 1m 47.265s

WITHDREW
20 Rosset BR
Tyrrell 026-Ford V10 (injured in practice) no time

RACE CLASSIFICATION

Pos	Driver	Nat	Car	Laps	Time
1	Mika Hakkinen	FIN	McLaren MP4/13-Mercedes V10	45	1h20m47.984s
2	David Coulthard	GB	McLaren MP4/13-Mercedes V10	45	+0.426s
3	Jacques Villeneuve	CDN	Williams FW20-Mecachrome V10	45	+2.577s
4	Damon Hill	GB	Jordan 198-Mugen Honda V10	45	+7.185s
5	Michael Schumacher	D	Ferrari F300-Ferrari V10	45	+12.613s
6	Ralf Schumacher	D	Jordan 198-Mugen Honda V10	45	+29.738s
7	Giancarlo Fisichella	I	Benetton B198-Playlife V10	45	+31.026s
8	Eddie Irvine	GB	Ferrari F300-Ferrari V10	45	+31.649s
9	Heinz-Harald Frentzen	D	Williams FW20-Mecachrome V10	45	+32.784s
10	Jean Alesi	F	Sauber C17-Petronas V10	45	+48.371s
11	Alexander Wurz	A	Benetton B198-Playlife V10	45	+57.994s
12	Jarno Trulli	I	Prost AP01-Peugeot V10		+1 lap
13	Tora Takagi	J	Tyrrell 026-Ford V10		+1 lap
14	Mika Salo	FIN	Arrows A19-Arrows V10		+1 lap
15	Olivier Panis	F	Prost AP01-Peugeot V10		+1 lap
16	Esteban Tuero	RA	Minardi M198-Ford V10		+2 laps

Retirements	Nat	Car	Laps	Reason
Johnny Herbert	GB	Sauber C17-Petronas V10	37	gearbox
Shinji Nakano	J	Minardi M198-Ford V10	36	gearbox
Rubens Barrichello	BR	Stewart SF-2-Ford V10	27	gearbox
Jos Verstappen	NL	Stewart SF-2-Ford V10	24	transmission
Pedro Diniz	BR	Arrows A19-Arrows V10	2	throttle

FASTEST LAP D Coulthard 1m46.116s lap 17 (143.830 mph/231.471kmh)

DRIVERS' CHAMPIONSHIP

Mika Hakkinen	76
Michael Schumacher	60
David Coulthard	42
Eddie Irvine	32
Alexander Wurz	17
Jacques Villeneuve	16
Giancarlo Fisichella	15
Heinz-Harald Frentzen	8
Rubens Barrichello	4
Ralf Schumacher	4
Jean Alesi	3
Damon Hill	3
Mika Salo	3
Pedro Diniz	1
Johnny Herbert	1
Jan Magnussen	1

CONSTRUCTORS' CHAMPIONSHIP

McLaren-Mercedes	118
Ferrari	92
Benetton-Playlife	32
Williams-Mecachrome	24
Jordan-Mugen Honda	7
Stewart-Ford	5
Arrows	4
Sauber-Petronas	4

anniversaries in 1998

November 7, **Ayrton Senna** won a grand prix for the 41st and final time (below).

10 years ago

Enzo Ferrari passed away on **August 14**, aged 90.

Ayrton Senna clinched the first of his three world titles in Japan on **October 30**.

Alain Prost scored the last F1 win for a turbocharged engine on **November 13** in Australia.

5 years ago

The South African circuit of **Kyalami** staged its last F1 race on **March 14**. . . though it is tipped for an imminent return to the F1 calendar.

June 15 marked the fifth anniversary of **James Hunt**'s untimely death, aged 45 (above).

Alain Prost scored the last of his 51 grand prix victories at Hockenheim on July 25. Shortly afterwards, on August 15, **Damon Hill** (above, middle) scored his first F1 win, in Budapest. At the end of the year, on

Niki Lauda gave the **Brabham** fan-car its only win in the 1978 Swedish GP on **June 17** (below). The controversial machine was banned thereafter.

On **March 4** future world champion **Keke**

15 years ago

Long Beach staged its final F1 race on **March 27**. McLaren driver **John Watson** scored what was to be the last grand prix victory of his career. It was a typical Watson performance; he carved through the field after starting 22nd.

Tyrrell scored its last F1 win on **June 5**, courtesy of Michele Alboreto (top) in Detroit.

20 years ago

Arrows appeared in grand prix racing for the first time, in Brazil. **Riccardo Patrese** finished 10th on the team's race debut on **January 29**.

Rosberg started a world championship race for the first time, in South Africa. It was an event that marked the final F1 start for **Hesketh**, the marque that helped guide **James Hunt** to prominence.

Nelson Piquet (left) lined up for his first grand prix at Hockenheim on **July 30**, driving for Ensign.

Lotus team-mates **Ronnie Peterson** and **Mario Andretti** scored the last grand prix wins of their career, in Austria (**August 13**) and Holland (**August 27**) respectively. Peterson would crash heavily at the start of the Italian GP on September 10 and succumbed to his injuries the following day.

Gilles Villeneuve scored his first grand prix victory in Canada on October 8 (left).

25 years ago

On **June 3 James Hunt** started a grand prix for the first time, at Monaco in **Hesketh** Racing's March.

Ronnie Peterson (below) scored his first GP win for Lotus in France on **July 1**.

30 years ago

Jim Clark died while driving for Lotus in an F2 race at Hockenheim. **April 7** went down as one of the darkest days in the history of the sport.

The **Matra** company's maiden F1 engine made its first start at Monaco on **May 26**. The French company scored its first F1 win at Zandvoort on **June 23** 1968 thanks to **Jackie Stewart**, whose Matra chassis was Cosworth powered (above).

McLaren Cars scored its first F1 win in Belgium on **June 9**. It was also company founder **Bruce McLaren**'s last grand prix triumph as a driver (above, left).

Mika Hakkinen (flying at Australia in '93, right) was born on **September 28**.

Graham Hill clinched his second world title in Mexico on **November 3**.

40 years ago

On **January 19 1958 Stirling Moss** (right) gave **Cooper Cars** and **Climax** engines their first grand prix victory. His success in Argentina was also the first-ever world championship triumph for a rear-engined F1 machine.

On **May 18 Lotus** appeared in a grand prix for the first time, at Monaco. One of the team's drivers was also an F1 newcomer: **Graham Hill**. Hill qualified for the race, which was more than one Connaught driver managed to do: **Bernie Ecclestone** was slowest of all in practice, though his mastery of F1 has improved with time.

Juan Manuel Fangio started his final grand prix on **July 6**, at Reims (right). He finished fourth in a **Maserati** 250F. The race was won by **Mike Hawthorn**, his final F1 success.

Hawthorn's bosom buddy **Peter Collins** (above) perished at the Nürburgring on **August 3**. Hawthorn went on to retire from the sport at the end of the year, after becoming the first Briton to clinch the title on **October 19**.

45 years ago

Hawthorn scored his very first grand prix win, at Reims on **July 5**. **Nigel Mansell** (above right) missed out on all the excitement; he was born a few weeks too late, on **August 8**.

50 years ago

Current team owner **Eddie Jordan** (right) was born on **March 30**. Future Renault and Ferrari F1 star **René Arnoux** arrived on **July 4** and 1982 world champion **Keke Rosberg** made his debut on **December 6**.

70 years ago

Wolfgang von Trips (above) was born on **May 4**. The German aristocrat was on course to become his country's first F1 champion when he crashed fatally at Monza in 1961. Germany would have to wait another 33 years.

Lotus founder **Colin Chapman** (above, talking to driver Jim Clark) was born on **May 19**.

75 years ago
"And here comes **Murray Walker**" (above right) – making a microphone-free entrance into the world on **October 10**.

80 years ago
Double world champion of the Fifties **Alberto Ascari** (shown right at Silverstone, 1948) was born on **July 13**.

100 years ago
On **February 18 1898** Mr and Mrs **Ferrari** chose to call their new-born son **Enzo**. He went on to have a passing interest in motor racing, the fruits of which endure today.

Beaten by Ferrari to the maternity ward by a few months, **Luigi Fagioli** popped into the world on **June 9**. Third in the inaugural world championship in 1950, the Italian sulked massively after Alfa Romeo asked him to hand his car to Fangio and take over the team leader's troubled machine in the following year's French GP. The two were eventually credited with joint first and 11th places, but after his only F1 'win' Fagioli never again drove in a grand prix.

McLaren-Mercedes chiefs Norbert Haug and Ron Dennis (below) discuss where they can get hold of the Ladybird Book of F1 Strategy after the virtuosity of Michael Schumacher had combined with some sharp tactical thinking to conjure up a victory from nothing (right).

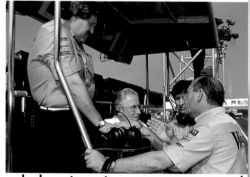

bold strategy – and a dash of genius from behind the wheel – combined to upset the form book as schuey added a little fizz to the title race

marlboro magyar

=nagydíj

Budapest is a colourful city of many contrasts. Quality restaurants nestle alongside seedy strip joints. New Mercedes-Benzes mingle in the traffic with erratically driven 15-year-old Wartburgs. String quartets in top-class eateries can switch at the drop of a hat (and with a little persuasion, admittedly) from a restful Strauss waltz to the theme from *Match of the Day*.

Not far down the road from all of this, there was another conspicuous clash of styles. While McLaren was plugging along conservatively on a two-stop strategy favoured by the majority of those in the Hungarian Grand Prix, Ferrari adopted an aggressive three-stop plan which, ultimately, left the hotly-tipped Silver Arrows in knots.

And McLaren appeared not to notice it coming. There seemed to be little danger in the early stages, when Mika Hakkinen and

David Coulthard led the way as Michael Schumacher settled in third place. But it was all to be decided by the second round of pit stops. Ferrari brought Schuey in early, gave him a reduced fuel load and sent him out in search of a miracle. And with Schumacher going along at one hell of a rate, McLaren opted to bring second-placed Coulthard in first – even though Hakkinen was far enough ahead of Schumacher to have retained the lead, and therefore vital track position, if the Finn had stopped at that point.

By the time Hakkinen came in, it was too late to stop the Prancing Horse which was now bolting. The Finn was out of the pits after Schumacher had sped into an unexpected lead, though of course the German would

buzzing in michael's ear was a message: "you have fuel for 19 laps to get a 25-second lead. do it."

old pals act

False dawn: The McLaren twins successfully kid lots of beer-swilling race fans that they are running in invincible mode (far left). Said fans were strangely delirious when this proved not to be the case.

Swiss watch: Pit stop time for Alesi (top left) as startled mechanics come to terms with the fact that both cars are a) still running and b) haven't hit each other.

Jacques and Hill: The reigning world champion chases his predecessor in the somewhat overlooked battle for third place (above right). The fact that Damon fared so well was offset by the fact that he had done even better the previous season. In an Arrows.

Rolling stones: Ralf Schumacher rediscovered some of his early-season form in Hungary (above left).

have to stop once more.

Buzzing in Michael's ear was a message from Ferrari's technical director and master strategist Ross Brawn: "You have fuel for 19 laps to get a 25-second lead. Do it." What he was really asking for was for his star turn to put in a string of 19 qualifying laps.

He was told to do it. . . and he did. Despite a momentary wobble at the final corner on lap 51, which cost him a couple of seconds as he ran wide, he was far enough ahead by lap 62 that he was able to refuel and return for the final 15 laps with fresh tyres and his lead intact.

It had been a tactical masterstroke, although it might have been made harder had Hakkinen not started to suffer from handling trouble. On the same lap as Schuey's only mistake of the afternoon, indeed, Mika pulled over to let Coulthard have a pop at the leader,

A COUPLE of years ago a straight fight between Jacques Villeneuve and Damon Hill was usually something in the TV spotlight – because it was almost inevitably that for the race lead.

But things have moved on since they were Williams team-mates. By Hungary Jacques was in the final stages of his contract, as he prepared to join the new British American Racing team, and Damon had long since been edged out of the nest. Here, however, their fight was for third place (once Hakkinen had slumped out of the picture) – and that was a sign of encouragement for the once familiar sparring partners.

Hill had qualified fourth and Villeneuve sixth, but in the end it was the Canadian's policy of running for longer on harder-compound tyres which allowed him to erode Damon's early advantage after the second round of pit stops. And once he was ahead he pulled away as Hill was left to fend off the second Williams of the slightly feverish Heinz-Harald Frentzen.

"The car just seemed to get better as the race went on," said Villeneuve, after his second straight podium finish. "And of all the tracks this season the Hungaroring was expected to suit our car least, so I'm especially pleased."

Hill was upbeat, too, even though this was the first time he had finished outside the top two in Hungary since he placed 11th in 1992 (and given that he was in a Brabham at the time, that was a pretty spectacular effort, too).

Budapest was not supposed to suit Jordan, either, but after an eight-race drought the team had picked up its fourth consecutive helping of points.

"It was a strong, competitive showing," said Damon, "and if we can do it here, of all places, it's got to look good for the rest of the season."

Even he could not have known what lay just around the corner, however.

spaced out **invaders**

THE fact that Eddie Irvine's Ferrari had been an early casualty with gearbox failure mattered not a jot to the massed ranks bearing allegiance to the Prancing Horse.

The overwhelming majority had eyes for only one man and their thunderous cries of "Schumi! Schumi!" would have been just about audible from the centre of Baltimore, never mind Budapest.

Their passion was not as much a problem as their impatience, however. From the moment Schumacher crossed the line, the tall debris fences began to creak as the fans stormed up and over and onto a track on which a race was still taking place. And that much should have been obvious even to the most drunken of a brigade in which many were the worse for beer.

Tyrrell driver Tora Takagi, in his first season of European racing, could not believe his eyes.

"It was scary," said Takagi, accustomed to the unfailing politeness of appreciative race fans in Japan.

"I got to the back of the circuit and there were people all over the track. I was lucky not to hit anyone."

In the past the FIA has taken a dim view of such disturbances. Silverstone had to take tough action in the Mansell years. Monza and Imola have had to plea for common sense from the tifosi.

And Le Mans was threatened with a ban unless the crowd could wait 24 hours and ten minutes (rather than 24 hours and two seconds) before the traditional track invasion.

For all that Budapest is popular with F1 insiders, however, the circuit itself would not be regarded as a major loss in the event of punitive action being taken.

While the 1998 race was tactically fascinating, the fact remained that all the significant overtaking was once again the result of pit stops.

Seeing someone draft past Hakkinen's stricken McLaren was hardly the stuff to set the nerves jangling.

Flare play: Punters begin to get steamed up as Schuey sneaks into contention (top). A moody piece of camera artistry earns Jacques Villeneuve a second appearance within the same report (above).

but there wasn't much the Scot could do. Schumacher admitted, afterwards, that the latest Goodyear race tyres were a step forward.

"I was surprised at how much Michael was able to get from his car," said Coulthard, who was three seconds per lap slower until Schumacher backed off in the final stages. "On our tyres we were okay for a couple of laps and then it started to be hard work."

At the start of an afternoon on which he had expected to extend his 16-point championship lead, the ill-handling Hakkinen dropped away to finish sixth and his margin of superiority was down to just seven points.

"It felt to me like I had done about 60 qualifying laps," beamed Schumacher after-wards. From where we were sitting, that looked about right.

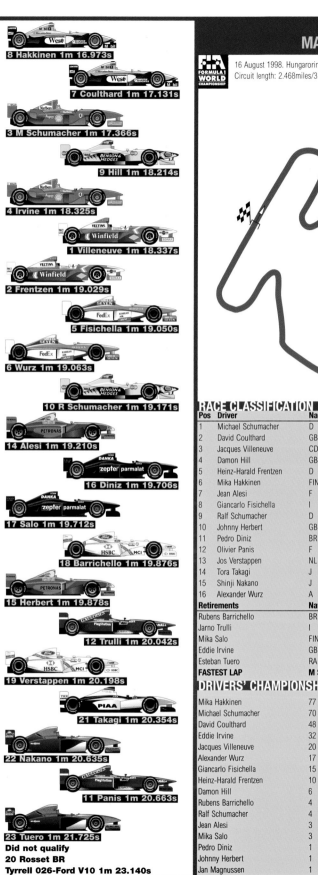

8 Hakkinen 1m 16.973s

7 Coulthard 1m 17.131s

3 M Schumacher 1m 17.366s

9 Hill 1m 18.214s

4 Irvine 1m 18.325s

1 Villeneuve 1m 18.337s

2 Frentzen 1m 19.029s

5 Fisichella 1m 19.050s

6 Wurz 1m 19.063s

10 R Schumacher 1m 19.171s

14 Alesi 1m 19.210s

16 Diniz 1m 19.706s

17 Salo 1m 19.712s

18 Barrichello 1m 19.876s

15 Herbert 1m 19.878s

12 Trulli 1m 20.042s

19 Verstappen 1m 20.198s

21 Takagi 1m 20.354s

22 Nakano 1m 20.635s

11 Panis 1m 20.663s

23 Tuero 1m 21.725s

Did not qualify
20 Rosset BR
Tyrrell 026-Ford V10 1m 23.140s

16 August 1998. Hungaroring, Mogyorod, near Budapest
Circuit length: 2.468miles/3.972km

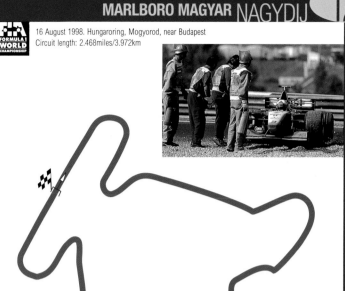

RACE CLASSIFICATION

Pos	Driver	Nat	Car	Laps	Time
1	Michael Schumacher	D	Ferrari F300-Ferrari V10	77	1h45m25.550s
2	David Coulthard	GB	McLaren MP4/13-Mercedes V10	77	+9.433s
3	Jacques Villeneuve	CDN	Williams FW20-Mecachrome V10	77	+44.444s
4	Damon Hill	GB	Jordan 198-Mugen Honda V10	77	+55.076s
5	Heinz-Harald Frentzen	D	Williams FW20-Mecachrome V10	77	+56.510s
6	Mika Hakkinen	FIN	McLaren MP4/13-Mercedes V10		+1 lap
7	Jean Alesi	F	Sauber C17-Petronas V10		+1 lap
8	Giancarlo Fisichella	I	Benetton B198-Playlife V10		+1 lap
9	Ralf Schumacher	D	Jordan 198-Mugen Honda V10		+1 lap
10	Johnny Herbert	GB	Sauber C17-Petronas V10		+1 lap
11	Pedro Diniz	BR	Arrows A19-Arrows V10		+3 laps
12	Olivier Panis	F	Prost AP01-Peugeot V10		+3 laps
13	Jos Verstappen	NL	Stewart SF-2-Ford V10		+3 laps
14	Tora Takagi	J	Tyrrell 026-Ford V10		+3 laps
15	Shinji Nakano	J	Minardi M198-Ford V10		+3 laps
16	Alexander Wurz	A	Benetton B198-Playlife V10		+8 laps

Retirements	Nat	Car	Laps	Reason
Rubens Barrichello	BR	Stewart SF-2-Ford V10	54	gearbox
Jarno Trulli	I	Prost AP01-Peugeot V10	28	engine
Mika Salo	FIN	Arrows A19-Arrows V10	18	hydraulics
Eddie Irvine	GB	Ferrari F300-Ferrari V10	13	gearbox
Esteban Tuero	RA	Minardi M198-Ford V10	13	gearbox

FASTEST LAP M Schumacher 1m19.286s lap 60 (112.064mph/180.350kmh)

DRIVERS' CHAMPIONSHIP

Mika Hakkinen	77
Michael Schumacher	70
David Coulthard	48
Eddie Irvine	32
Jacques Villeneuve	20
Alexander Wurz	17
Giancarlo Fisichella	15
Heinz-Harald Frentzen	10
Damon Hill	6
Rubens Barrichello	4
Ralf Schumacher	4
Jean Alesi	3
Mika Salo	3
Pedro Diniz	1
Johnny Herbert	1
Jan Magnussen	1

CONSTRUCTORS' CHAMPIONSHIP

McLaren-Mercedes	125
Ferrari	102
Benetton-Playlife	32
Williams-Mecachrome	30
Jordan-Mugen Honda	10
Stewart-Ford	5
Arrows	4
Sauber-Petronas	4

foster's
belgian
grand prix

the weather
was dull, but there
wasn't a moment to
match it as damon
hill gave jordan its
first-ever f1 success
in the most bizarre
race since stirling
moss was in shorts

Water cannon: Hill
successfully manages
to avoid running into
any stray McLarens
and is rewarded with
the 22nd victory of
his F1 career (left). A
question for gamblers:
what odds could you
have got on two Jordan
drivers and one from
Sauber (above) making
it onto the podium?

Turn back a couple of pages and you

will find Damon Hill predicting that things were going to get better for Jordan in the final races of the year.

It is nothing new for racing drivers to bluster on thus, but no one could possibly have predicted quite how things would turn out in Belgium.

Hill, the so-called missing ingredient in the Jordan recipe, finally delivered the team the first of the grand prix wins it had been promising itself since its brash arrival in F1 in 1991. To complete Jordan's extraordinary day Ralf Schumacher finished second – but the most remarkable statistic was that there were far bigger stories to emerge from the weekend than a mere Jordan 1-2.

It all started on lap one. Or rather, it didn't start.

In the kind of damp, murky conditions which typify Spa in August (as well as every other month, to be fair), Hill was left cursing a bad start which appeared to have wasted his excellent third place on the grid. Fortunately for Damon, however, his start wasn't quite bad enough to drop him into the clutches of one of the biggest F1 pile-ups since

records began.

It commenced as the field exited the La Source hairpin before the plunge to Eau Rouge. Eddie Irvine clipped David Coulthard and the Scot's McLaren veered across the track and slammed into the concrete wall in front of the old pits before rebounding into the path of most of the field.

The after-effects were a bit like those you get when you become bored after you have crashed while playing a racing simulation on a computer. Go on, admit it – you have deliberately driven the wrong way around a track causing spiteful havoc.

In all 12 cars – those of Coulthard, Irvine, Jarno Trulli, Mika Salo, Ricardo Rosset, Olivier Panis, Rubens Barrichello, Toranosuke Takagi, Pedro Diniz, Shinji Nakano, Alexander Wurz and Johnny Herbert – were enmeshed in a torrent of flying wheels and wishbones. Miraculously, no one was hurt, though

the most remarkable statistic was that there were far bigger stories to emerge from the weekend than a mere Jordan 1-2

rocky
98

Ire starter: Schumacher brushes Hakkinen (far left) as the field attempts to get away for a second time with slightly less mass destruction. The clash spelt the end of the race for the Finn.

Campaign for real Alesi: The Frenchman showed his mettle in the deplorable conditions and gave Sauber its first podium finish of the year (top left).

Heady Jordan: EJ tries to persuade Sly Stallone that his new status as a grand prix winner merits him a walk-on part in the new F1 movie (above right).

Special bruise: Mika Salo escaped this wreck (above left) with nothing worse than a damaged car.

SYLVESTER Stallone was a familiar visitor to F1 paddocks in 1998 as he researched his forthcoming Hollywood racing epic. And for a moment one could have been forgiven for thinking that the punchy looking chap in red overalls was on a Stallone set.

But this was all too real as a furious Michael Schumacher launched himself into the McLaren pit at Spa. The German decided that David Coulthard had deliberately caused them to collide at enormous speed in the pouring rain and went to scream as much in the Scot's general direction after an accident which had cost Schumacher the chance of leading the championship for the first time all season.

While tempers raged, however, Ferrari number two Eddie Irvine was a voice of reason as he pointed out that Coulthard is simply not the sort of bloke who behaves as his team-mate was alleging. "David is not like that," he said, "and I don't think there is anyone in the field who would cause anything like this on purpose."

Schumacher accused Coulthard of having slowed down in a dangerous place; Coulthard pointed out that he had backed off – as Ferrari sporting director Jean Todt had been imploring McLaren to ask him to – and kept to the right on the approach to Pouhon corner in order to let the leader pass. "I stayed to the side of the track and the next thing I know he was running into the back of me," he said.

The stewards summoned both men and, after studying telemetry from Coulthard's car, deduced that it had been an unfortunate racing accident and that the Scot had done nothing to provoke it.

At Monza, two weeks later, Schumacher and Coulthard sat down together to make their peace (in public, at least).

More than anything, however, the incident simply amplified the perils of racing in heavy rain. The victims this time were the best driver of his era and one of the most level-headed F1 racers of any generation.

In conditions as bad as they were at Spa, no one is ever immune.

Barrichello banged his arm and did not take the restart. He was joined on the sidelines by Rosset, Panis and Salo, simply because teams did not have enough cars to go round (Arrows and Williams had already lost one apiece when Salo and Villeneuve had massive qualifying shunts at the top of Eau Rouge).

Hill made a much better fist of the restart and led the field away as Mika Hakkinen was pitched into a terminal spin by Schumacher. As Wurz and Coulthard skated off together on the first lap it was clear that the Bridgestone runners were not as comfortable in the ghastly conditions as their Goodyear counterparts.

Hill led for eight laps until the inevitable Schumacher emerged through the spray to take the lead, and thereafter the two of them were in a league of their own. . . until the German smashed into Coulthard as he attempted to put him a lap down.

It was by no means a unique situation in the blinding spray and when Fisichella reduced his Benetton to component form (using Nakano's Minardi as a launching pad) the Safety Car came out while the debris was swept away.

113

voyage to the F1 summit the eddie jordan way

1991: Neat car mated to Cosworth V8 scored points in Canada, only its fifth race. Team went on to finish fifth in the constructors' championship. Highlights of year included giving Michael Schumacher his F1 debut in Spa; lowlights included having his contract snaffled by Benetton before the next race in Italy. . . and regular driver Bertrand Gachot being jailed after using a pepper spray during a row with a London cabbie. Also gave 1999 Williams driver Alex Zanardi his first F1 start, at Jerez.

1992: Free engines from Yamaha offered financial salvation. . . but no performance. "I could have done with *The Sunday Times* at Hockenheim because the straights went on for so bloody long," says Mauricio Gugelmin. Team 11th in the constructors' championship after scraping a point from the last race.

1993: Arrival of Hart V10 and youth of Rubens Barrichello provide fresh impetus and there is much promise, if few results. No stability in second seat, where Eddie Irvine emerges as best of five drivers tried. The Ulsterman is thumped by Senna after a lively first race in Japan, where both cars finish in the top six to score the team's only points of the season (which means a step up to 10th).

1994: Irvine banned for three races for causing a pile-up in Brazil. Barrichello scores first podium finish in Pacific GP at Aida and gives team its first pole after a bold tyre gamble at Spa. The Brazilian finishes sixth in the drivers' championship and Jordan is fifth best team.

1995: Potent new engine partner in Peugeot but decent results

are few and far between – except in Canada, where Barrichello is second and Irvine third. Eddie signs a new contract late in the season and is then promptly sold to Ferrari. Team slips to sixth in championship.

1996: Martin Brundle replaces Irvine and has a huge accident in Melbourne – his first race with Jordan since he drove for their F3 team in 1983. Points scored in nine of the 16 races and team is back up to fifth in the constructors' table.

1997: All change. Barrichello goes to Stewart; Brundle becomes a TV commentator; Giancarlo Fisichella and Ralf Schumacher develop a nasty habit of driving into each other in the team's final season with Peugeot. The Italian is third in Canada and second in Belgium; Ralf is third in Argentina after shovelling his team-mate aside. The team unsurprisingly, is fifth in the. . . stop us if you've heard this before.

1998: Peugeot replaced by Mugen Honda V10. Damon Hill is snapped up to replace Fisichella. The year starts as a complete cataclysm but things improve at Silverstone, and not just because EJ has to cancel his traditional party to rush off to the World Cup final. Then there are miraculous goings-on in Belgium, albeit mostly shrouded in spray.

Jordan bankers: EJ celebrates (above left) the fruits of a career in which he has endured the highs of Schumacher's F1 debut (top right), the lows of a Yamaha engine deal (centre right) and a first F1 pole with Barrichello in 1994 (below right), at the same circuit where the victory duck was finally broken.

After the restart Hill and the surviving Schumacher had Alesi's Sauber for close company. The team issued orders not to jeopardise their position by racing and Ralf sulked for the rest of the day as Damon stroked to the 22nd win of his career, albeit his first in anything other than a Williams.

Behind the unusual combination of two Jordans and

a Sauber on the podium, Frentzen took fourth, Diniz fifth and Prost scored its first point of the year thanks to Trulli. The repaired cars of Coulthard and Nakano were classified, several light years behind.

A word of praise for Esteban Tuero and Jos Verstappen: they were the only two among the retirements who didn't actually crash.

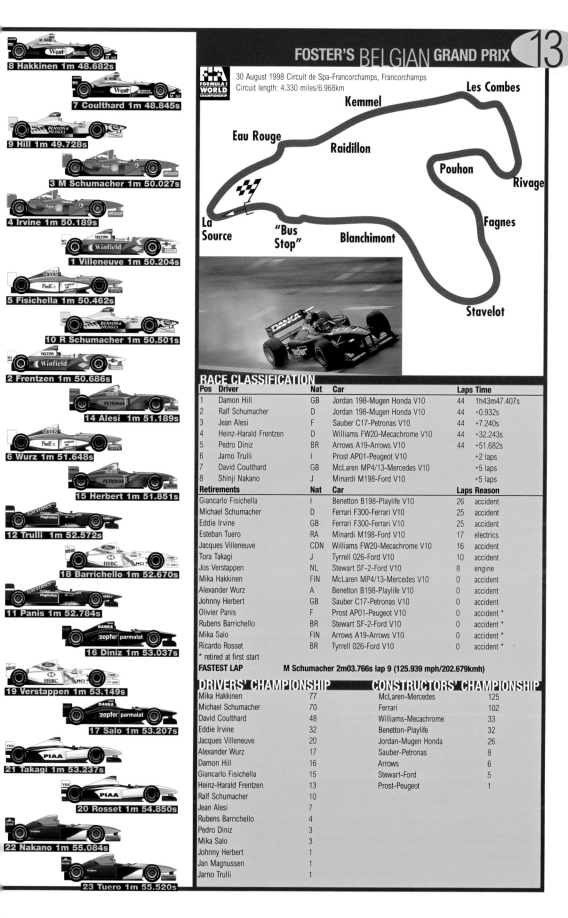

8 Hakkinen 1m 48.682s

7 Coulthard 1m 48.845s

9 Hill 1m 49.728s

3 M Schumacher 1m 50.027s

4 Irvine 1m 50.189s

1 Villeneuve 1m 50.204s

5 Fisichella 1m 50.462s

10 R Schumacher 1m 50.501s

2 Frentzen 1m 50.686s

14 Alesi 1m 51.189s

6 Wurz 1m 51.648s

15 Herbert 1m 51.851s

12 Trulli 1m 52.572s

18 Barrichello 1m 52.670s

11 Panis 1m 52.784s

16 Diniz 1m 53.037s

19 Verstappen 1m 53.149s

17 Salo 1m 53.207s

21 Takagi 1m 53.237s

20 Rosset 1m 54.850s

22 Nakano 1m 55.084s

23 Tuero 1m 55.520s

30 August 1998 Circuit de Spa-Francorchamps, Francorchamps
Circuit length: 4.330 miles/6.968km

Les Combes
Kemmel
Eau Rouge
Raidillon
Pouhon
Rivage
La Source
"Bus Stop"
Blanchimont
Fagnes
Stavelot

RACE CLASSIFICATION

Pos	Driver	Nat	Car	Laps	Time
1	Damon Hill	GB	Jordan 198-Mugen Honda V10	44	1h43m47.407s
2	Ralf Schumacher	D	Jordan 198-Mugen Honda V10	44	+0.932s
3	Jean Alesi	F	Sauber C17-Petronas V10	44	+7.240s
4	Heinz-Harald Frentzen	D	Williams FW20-Mecachrome V10	44	+32.243s
5	Pedro Diniz	BR	Arrows A19-Arrows V10	44	+51.682s
6	Jarno Trulli	I	Prost AP01-Peugeot V10		+2 laps
7	David Coulthard	GB	McLaren MP4/13-Mercedes V10		+5 laps
8	Shinji Nakano	J	Minardi M198-Ford V10		+5 laps

Retirements	Nat	Car	Laps	Reason
Giancarlo Fisichella	I	Benetton B198-Playlife V10	26	accident
Michael Schumacher	D	Ferrari F300-Ferrari V10	25	accident
Eddie Irvine	GB	Ferrari F300-Ferrari V10	25	accident
Esteban Tuero	RA	Minardi M198-Ford V10	17	electrics
Jacques Villeneuve	CDN	Williams FW20-Mecachrome V10	16	accident
Tora Takagi	J	Tyrrell 026-Ford V10	10	accident
Jos Verstappen	NL	Stewart SF-2-Ford V10	8	engine
Mika Hakkinen	FIN	McLaren MP4/13-Mercedes V10	0	accident
Alexander Wurz	A	Benetton B198-Playlife V10	0	accident
Johnny Herbert	GB	Sauber C17-Petronas V10	0	accident
Olivier Panis	F	Prost AP01-Peugeot V10	0	accident *
Rubens Barrichello	BR	Stewart SF-2-Ford V10	0	accident *
Mika Salo	FIN	Arrows A19-Arrows V10	0	accident *
Ricardo Rosset	BR	Tyrrell 026-Ford V10	0	accident *

* retired at first start

FASTEST LAP   M Schumacher 2m03.766s lap 9 (125.939 mph/202.679kmh)

DRIVERS' CHAMPIONSHIP

Mika Hakkinen	77
Michael Schumacher	70
David Coulthard	48
Eddie Irvine	32
Jacques Villeneuve	20
Alexander Wurz	17
Damon Hill	16
Giancarlo Fisichella	15
Heinz-Harald Frentzen	13
Ralf Schumacher	10
Jean Alesi	7
Rubens Barrichello	4
Pedro Diniz	3
Mika Salo	3
Johnny Herbert	1
Jan Magnussen	1
Jarno Trulli	1

CONSTRUCTORS' CHAMPIONSHIP

McLaren-Mercedes	125
Ferrari	102
Williams-Mecachrome	33
Benetton-Playlife	32
Jordan-Mugen Honda	26
Sauber-Petronas	8
Arrows	6
Stewart-Ford	5
Prost-Peugeot	1

69° gran premio campari

d'italia

they came,
they saw, they
faltered – and
so ferrari
conquered. the
prancing horse
profited from
mclaren's misery
to score a first
1-2 at monza
since 1988

Prancing hoarse: The crowd goes ballistic and waves around a flag the size of Luxembourg as their current hero speeds past (left). The 600 refers to the number of grands prix Ferrari has taken part in rather than the number of drivers Schuey has shoved off (top). The Schumacher brothers (with Irvine, above) are the first ever to stand together on an F1 podium. Bizarrely, Ralf looks happier than he did when he finished second in Spa.

the tifosi, more
enthusiastic
than a juventus
penalty claim
at the best of
times, went
berserk

Monza. Track of motor racing legend, mecca of grand prix fans, theatre of dreams. Or your very worst nightmare. . . if you were Mika Hakkinen.

The world championship leader came to the Italian Grand Prix knowing that a good result would bring the crown ever nearer. But he left dead level with Michael Schumacher after the German took one of the very best victories in his glittering career.

Just to rub it in, Eddie Irvine followed him home to give Ferrari its first 1-2 at Monza in 10 years. The tifosi, more enthusiastic than a Juventus penalty claim at the best of times, went berserk.

The Scuderia came to its home track prepared for a hiding: after all, the powerful, slippery McLaren-Mercs had given Schumacher and Irvine a real drubbing at Hockenheim, the other track on the calendar which most resembles Monza.

This time it was different: perhaps it was tyres, perhaps the engine, or perhaps Ferrari was just surfing a wave of confidence on the back of a sea of adoring tifosi. Schumacher took a crowd-pleasing pole, with Jacques Villeneuve's Williams as a buffer between him and anything silver. Yet even when Hakkinen and Coulthard piled into the lead, McLaren was to prove the agent of its own demise.

Troubled by poor chassis balance, Hakkinen was quick to let his team-mate play the hare. And Coulthard obliged. But the Scot's rampant march into the distance was halted when his Mercedes engine blew, stranding him far enough from the pits to make the return walk uncomfortable, given that ardent Ferrari fans were baying for his blood post-Spa.

And worse was to follow for Woking's wounded. Schumacher had wasted little time

silver arrows need sharpening

RON Dennis likes to talk, expounding complex, quasi-philosophical theories in long streams of compound words. In Monza, though, he had no hesitation in mincing them. McLaren's boss was forthright: his team was throwing its world title away.

With the pendulum of points-scoring momentum powering in Ferrari's direction, Dennis wasn't about to damn his rival with faint praise. The Italians were back in contention because McLaren had underperformed, he said. And if it carried on like this, his team would end up bereft of silverware.

"If we fail to win the championship I'll be most unhappy with our efforts," admitted Dennis. "We have fought at every GP and sometimes we get it a bit wrong. Inevitably you pay the price."

There was little sign of any immediate Ferrari concessions. Schumacher had suffered just one terminal mechanical problem on his Prancing Horse all season – and that was a handful of laps into the opening race. Irvine's track record was equally blemish-free. Ferrari might have made remarkable strides in competitiveness, but they had been eclipsed by its genuinely fantastic reliability.

Compared to the Italians, the McLaren-Mercedes casualty list read like a golf score. Mechanical problems had stopped Hakkinen in Imola, Coulthard in Monaco and both drivers in Canada. A damper problem hindered Mika in Hungary, and when Coulthard ground to a tifosi-pleasing halt at Monza it brought Ferrari to within a too-close-for-comfort ten points of its main title rival.

Cue Dennis, grinding his teeth: "The races they've won are races we've lost and they've been there to collect.

"We've won more grands prix than anyone else and Michael Schumacher is a highly talented and motivated driver. But he has made mistakes this year and there is no reason why he won't make them again."

A couple of doors down the paddock, though, and Ferrari's sporting chief Jean Todt was teeing up a bite-sized riposte. "Every time we put McLaren under pressure things go well for us," he smirked.

Squeeze box: Hakkinen escaped Schumacher's attempts to force him to mate with a Williams at the start to take the early lead (far left). Not that it did him much good, mind.

Traffic master: Irvine treads carefully amongst those a lap in arrears in his attempt to score a few brownie points with a crowd that had eyes for approximately one Ferrari driver (top left).

Walk on the wild side: Less than ideal situations, number one in a series. After having alienated the not always entirely reasonable Schumacher fan club at Spa, Coulthard found himself having to walk within spitting distance after his leading McLaren blew up at Monza (above right).

Sauber cream: Alesi remains a hot favourite with the Italian crowds, though that has more to do with his Sicilian roots than his Swiss car. His fifth place (above left) was warmly received.

in dismissing Villeneuve and Irvine, and he was closing in on Hakkinen when the Finn plunged into the haze of smoke, oil and water from Coulthard's blow-up. Unsighted, he took to the grass at the Curva Grande – and that was all Schumacher needed to make a move which stuck at the first chicane.

Hakkinen was fighting a losing battle. He lost it with six laps to go, when his brake pedal went to the floor as he slowed for the chicane and he spun wildly through the gravel. He recovered – but with a very blunted Silver Arrow.

"I was having to use the gears to slow the car down," he said. "It is quite an experience to drive a Formula One car with no way of stopping it."

The upshot was that he had no way of stopping Irvine, either, as the Ulsterman relieved him of second place. Nor did he have an answer for Ralf Schumacher, who became the second half of the first brotherhood to

third place
cash course

ANYONE involved in F1 will tell you that victory is everything and that finishing second is worthless – until they talk to their accountants, that is.

McLaren and Ferrari were in a league of their own points-wise – the Prancing Horse alone had the same number of points as every other team bar its main rival post-Monza. But an equally ferocious battle was brewing behind them for third between Williams, Benetton and up-and-comer Jordan. And there was a lot more than pride at stake.

Bonus money paid out by grand prix ringmaster Bernie Ecclestone to the most successful teams – habitually the Big Four of McLaren, Ferrari, Williams and Benetton – is serious wedge. Getting anybody to tell you exactly how much is a bit like seeing a Minardi on pole: it doesn't happen. But conservative estimates suggested that Jordan – the team which had spent most of the Nineties banging on the Big Four's door – stood to make a cool £10 million in extra pay-outs from the grand prix prize fund if it could leap-frog its rivals for third.

What made the contest all the more fascinating was the fact that neither Williams nor Benetton could lay any claim to being on form. The world champion team had made patchy progress all season, while its colourful rival had suffered colourful fortunes. Giancarlo Fisichella and Alex Wurz had failed to score a single point since the British Grand Prix – the race at which, coincidentally enough, Jordan finally broke its 1998 duck.

The turnaround in fortunes for Eddie Jordan's men was perhaps the single most surprising facet of an exciting season, although the likes of McLaren's Ron Dennis were sceptical.

"I'm sure they wouldn't like to hear it, but the vast majority of the teams aren't there to take the fight to us," he said.

"Only two teams have been in an exceptionally strong position and when we make a mistake, instead of being four teams there to pick up the points there's one." In other words, Schumacher's Ferrari.

stand together on an F1 podium. But the unadulterated joy of the track invaders was reserved for Michael.

With the cars barely finished, fences and guardrails could no longer contain the tifosi as they swarmed across the track, making a bee-line to get close to Schumacher's exultant podium celebrations and nicking anything in their wake that wasn't firmly nailed down or locked away.

This was a red sea that Moses would have had a job parting – and a tide that, for an afternoon at least, seemed capable of washing McLaren away.

Glow, buddy, glow: Takagi lights up his brakes as he thrusts his Tyrrell towards a reasonably sensible ninth place (below). Future team-mates Frentzen and Hill lock up (top) during their battle for sixth, a contest won – incidentally – by the man Frank Williams sacked to make way for the German.

But maybe that was a tad unfair on another man who answered to the name Schumacher. While Damon Hill gave Jordan its first grand prix win at Spa, it was arguably Ralf who had been the vanguard of the team's renaissance – by scoring points in every race bar one since Silverstone.

Third at Monza matched his best-ever result and the timing was perfect. Before the next race, the badly-kept secret that he was on his way to Williams for 1999 was finally revealed. Ironic, then, that he stood between his new employer and a big bundle of cash in the meantime. . .

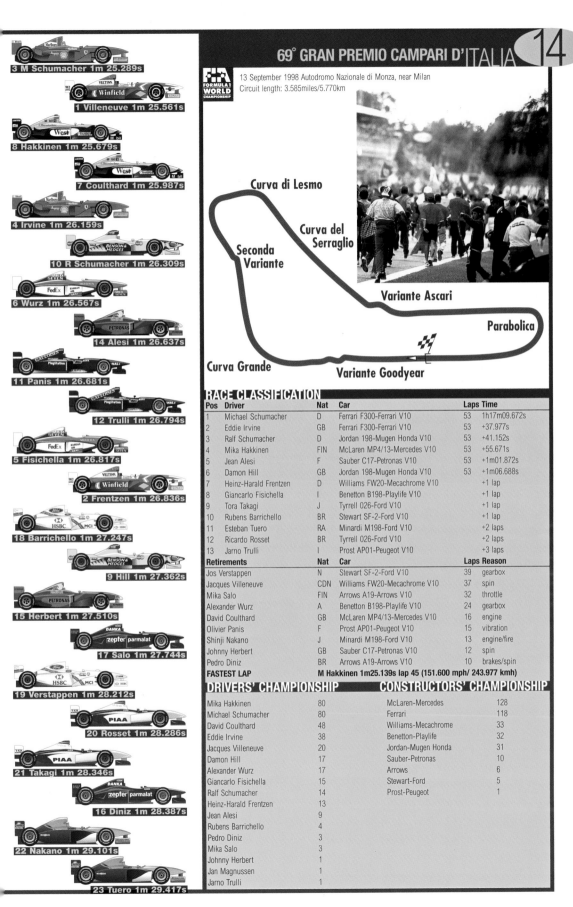

3 M Schumacher 1m 25.289s
1 Villeneuve 1m 25.561s
8 Hakkinen 1m 25.679s
7 Coulthard 1m 25.987s
4 Irvine 1m 26.159s
10 R Schumacher 1m 26.309s
6 Wurz 1m 26.567s
14 Alesi 1m 26.637s
11 Panis 1m 26.681s
12 Trulli 1m 26.794s
5 Fisichella 1m 26.817s
2 Frentzen 1m 26.836s
18 Barrichello 1m 27.247s
9 Hill 1m 27.362s
15 Herbert 1m 27.510s
17 Salo 1m 27.744s
19 Verstappen 1m 28.212s
20 Rosset 1m 28.286s
21 Takagi 1m 28.346s
16 Diniz 1m 28.387s
22 Nakano 1m 29.101s
23 Tuero 1m 29.417s

13 September 1998 Autodromo Nazionale di Monza, near Milan
Circuit length: 3.585miles/5.770km

Curva di Lesmo
Curva del Serraglio
Seconda Variante
Variante Ascari
Parabolica
Curva Grande
Variante Goodyear

RACE CLASSIFICATION

Pos	Driver	Nat	Car	Laps	Time
1	Michael Schumacher	D	Ferrari F300-Ferrari V10	53	1h17m09.672s
2	Eddie Irvine	GB	Ferrari F300-Ferrari V10	53	+37.977s
3	Ralf Schumacher	D	Jordan 198-Mugen Honda V10	53	+41.152s
4	Mika Hakkinen	FIN	McLaren MP4/13-Mercedes V10	53	+55.671s
5	Jean Alesi	F	Sauber C17-Petronas V10	53	+1m01.872s
6	Damon Hill	GB	Jordan 198-Mugen Honda V10	53	+1m06.688s
7	Heinz-Harald Frentzen	D	Williams FW20-Mecachrome V10		+1 lap
8	Giancarlo Fisichella	I	Benetton B198-Playlife V10		+1 lap
9	Tora Takagi	J	Tyrrell 026-Ford V10		+1 lap
10	Rubens Barrichello	BR	Stewart SF-2-Ford V10		+1 lap
11	Esteban Tuero	RA	Minardi M198-Ford V10		+2 laps
12	Ricardo Rosset	BR	Tyrrell 026-Ford V10		+2 laps
13	Jarno Trulli	I	Prost AP01-Peugeot V10		+3 laps

Retirements	Nat	Car	Laps	Reason
Jos Verstappen	N	Stewart SF-2-Ford V10	39	gearbox
Jacques Villeneuve	CDN	Williams FW20-Mecachrome V10	37	spin
Mika Salo	FIN	Arrows A19-Arrows V10	32	throttle
Alexander Wurz	A	Benetton B198-Playlife V10	24	gearbox
David Coulthard	GB	McLaren MP4/13-Mercedes V10	16	engine
Olivier Panis	F	Prost AP01-Peugeot V10	15	vibration
Shinji Nakano	J	Minardi M198-Ford V10	13	engine/fire
Johnny Herbert	GB	Sauber C17-Petronas V10	12	spin
Pedro Diniz	BR	Arrows A19-Arrows V10	10	brakes/spin

FASTEST LAP   M Hakkinen 1m25.139s lap 45 (151.600 mph/ 243.977 kmh)

DRIVERS' CHAMPIONSHIP

Mika Hakkinen	80
Michael Schumacher	80
David Coulthard	48
Eddie Irvine	38
Jacques Villeneuve	20
Damon Hill	17
Alexander Wurz	17
Giancarlo Fisichella	15
Ralf Schumacher	14
Heinz-Harald Frentzen	13
Jean Alesi	9
Rubens Barrichello	4
Pedro Diniz	3
Mika Salo	3
Johnny Herbert	1
Jan Magnussen	1
Jarno Trulli	1

CONSTRUCTORS' CHAMPIONSHIP

McLaren-Mercedes	128
Ferrari	118
Williams-Mecachrome	33
Benetton-Playlife	32
Jordan-Mugen Honda	31
Sauber-Petronas	10
Arrows	6
Stewart-Ford	5
Prost-Peugeot	1

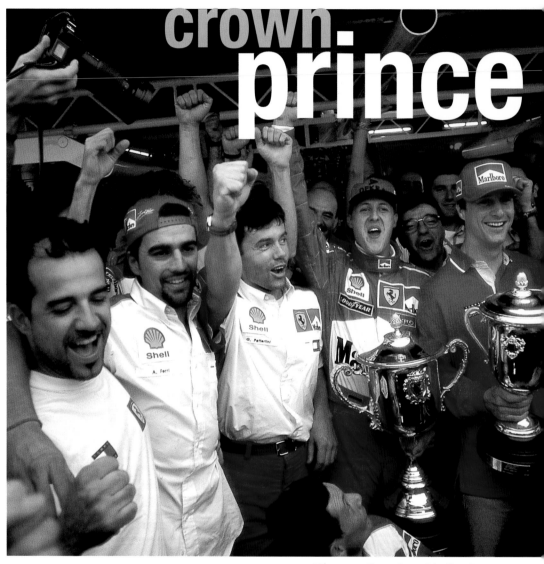

crown
prince

. . .or clown prince?
there were two
distinct sides of
michael schumacher
on parade throughout
the 1998 season

They say there is a thin line between genius and madness. In Michael Schumacher's case, make that badness.

Throughout his career, this granite-chinned 29-year-old German has been cast as the bad guy: arrogant, aggressive, willing to stop at nothing if it means victory. As a result, he started this season under greater scrutiny than ever before. Not least because in 1997's finale at Jerez Schumacher had tried, in vain, to barge Jacques Villeneuve off the road as the Williams driver made the move that sealed his world championship – and that had given his detractors plenty of ammunition.

If Schumacher started the year in the public

Fête train: Schumacher, Irvine and the Ferrari crew celebrate after taking an early lead in the Argentine Stock Car Championship (left).

Dark side of the man: The two sides of Schuey (above).

and Goodyear struggling to get its tyres onto the same performance plane as Bridgestone. And despite a recovery in terms of results, the Italian team never quite caught up with its arch-rival's technical superiority. Perhaps that's why we were privy to more Schumacher mistakes this year than in a long time.

Monaco, a track where the German had demonstrated true genius in the past, was a nightmare. Beaten by Hakkinen for speed and Benetton for strategy, Schumacher came off worst in a wheel-rubbing match with Alex Wurz and then crashed out while inexplicably trying to unlap himself. From Pedro Diniz.

For Schumacher, this was real boot-on-the-other-foot stuff – but perhaps a greater shock was in store in Austria. Faster than Hakkinen, he itched to get past the McLaren – but couldn't make a move stick before he ploughed through a gravel trap and ripped off the Ferrari's nose wing. And in the penultimate race, at the Nürburgring, he was simply given a taste of his own medicine by an in-form Hakkinen and McLaren's on-the-ball pit crew.

But did any of it suggest that the king's crown was slipping?

The big stumbling block for critics has always been a talent so evident that it is impossible to deny his mantle as the finest driver of his generation. He has often been described as a flawed genius in the mould of the late, great Ayrton Senna – and there were moments in 1998 when Schumacher's tactics were redolent of Senna at his worst.

Take Argentina, where his victory was tarnished by an uncompromising move on Coulthard. Consider his pot/black kettle altercations with Heinz-Harald Frentzen and Damon Hill in Canada. Most astonishing of all was Spa, where his attitude following his collision with Coulthard merged with a stubborn refusal to accept one iota of blame. And that was too much for Coulthard.

"All that happened in Argentina was that I came off worst, but Michael drove into the side of my car," said the Scot. "If people want to see drivers bashing into one another they should go to stock car races."

Sure, the Scot was biased, but his views were shared by others – including thrice world champion Jackie Stewart and FIA President

gaze, so did his team – albeit for a different reason. This year, said Ferrari, was the year in which it was going to land its first F1 title for drivers since The Buzzcocks were all the rage. Schumacher, armed with the technical "dream team" which brought him two world titles at Benetton, was the man to do the job. Yet even as Ferrari delivered this bold message, all people wanted to talk about to the knight in shining red armour was Jerez. Clearly, this campaign would bring pressure like none before. And there were times when it told.

Ferrari started under the cosh, with a car over a second a lap slower than McLaren's

Max Mosley, who admitted that Schumacher had gone too far after Spa. "His reaction was obviously over the top," he said, "but I am sure on mature reflection he would realise it was an error of judgement."

It's uncertain that Schumacher agreed, although he did at least later make peace with Coulthard.

So where does all this leave Schumacher? Trying to make a pattern from a few isolated errors in the course of a season might appear over-zealous – but in the past such lapses have been fewer and further between. Even Ferrari technical chief Ross Brawn – a staunch supporter of the German – admitted he was surprised that it was Hakkinen, rather than his more experienced title rival, who had handled the pressure at the A1-Ring best. With Schumacher having agreed an 80 million dollar four-year contract with Ferrari before the race, could that have been a one-off case of Schumacher taking his eye off the ball? Or a flickering indication of something more symbolic – a shifting of the F1 balance of power from Michael to Mika? As the season drew to a close, the questions still hung in the air.

Schumacher couldn't see what all the fuss was about. "The only real mistake I made was in Austria," he said. "I pushed very hard to keep on the pace and I missed the entry to a corner. But that had something to do with a pair of cars in front of me which are rather difficult to beat.

most astonishing of all was spa, where his attitude following his collision with coulthard merged with a stubborn refusal to accept one iota of blame

Smiles per hour: A couple of half-decent F1 drivers do their best to pretend that they are enjoying a press conference (above).

"I don't think I made more mistakes because of the pressure from McLaren. With the possible exception of the first part of 1994 I have always been competing against drivers in better cars. We have had to compete by using team work and going our own way."

He's got a point. Consider, too, some alternative evidence.

If the season started badly for Ferrari, it wasn't until the German Grand Prix that things hit rock bottom. The high-speed Hockenheim track suited McLaren like no other: all weekend the Ferraris looked out of sorts, with Schumacher struggling to keep his wayward machine in the frame for a points finish.

And if the F300 could be that bad, how on earth was Schumacher mounting a championship challenge?

The Hungarian Grand Prix, two weeks later, provided all the answers. Trailing the Silver Arrows once more, Schumacher took the whip to his Prancing Horse to devastating effect. His startling pace not only saw off Hakkinen and Coulthard, it underlined Schumacher's place in the grand prix pecking order.

"This freak comes along and it's going to be 20 years before anybody gets close," hooted Eddie Irvine on the eve of Suzuka. "And he's never driven the best car. God help everyone else if our Ferrari is as good as the McLaren next year – and I think that's possible."

Ferrari's rivals had better hope he's wrong. For all the mistakes, there was proof enough in 1998 that there really is no one else quite like Schuey.

the case for the prosecution

ARGENTINA

Just three races after Jerezgate, Schumacher is in the dock for barging David Coulthard out of the lead in Buenos Aires. He goes on to win and Coulthard makes a reasoned plea for the powers-that-be to define what constitutes an acceptable overtaking manoeuvre. The stewards are unmoved.

CANADA

Ferrari's second win of the year is clouded when Schumacher – who claims he was unsighted – pulls out of the pit lane and lunges towards Heinz-Harald Frentzen, pushing the Williams onto the grass at 180mph. The Ferrari pilot later apologises – but only after accusing Damon Hill of trying to kill him during a heated mid-race battle for second.

Belgian shocks: Schuey was on course for victory when he popped into his local Spa (above). . . until a clash with Coulthard brought out the worst in the German.

SPA

Notorious collision with David Coulthard while trying to lap the McLaren pilot in gales of spray. Storms into McLaren garage and accuses the Scot of "trying to effing kill me" upon his return to the pits. Half backs down at much-publicised handshake two weeks later at Monza.

. . .and the defence

Wash'n'go: Although he was outpaced in the early stages at Silverstone, Schuey came into his own shortly after he had lapped the Oxford boat crew (right).

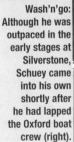

SILVERSTONE

Pouring rain is meat and drink to Schumacher. He might have been lucky to go unpunished in the great yellow flag fiasco, but it shouldn't overshadow a consummate display of artistry at the wheel. Where all the others spin, Schumacher simply wins.

HUNGARY

A race Ferrari shouldn't have won. But they do, thanks to a bold pit stop strategy that only Schumacher could have driven hard and fast enough to make work. "You have fuel for 19 laps to build a 25-second lead. Do it." That's the order from technical chief Ross Brawn. So that's exactly what Michael does.

MONZA

Awful start; brilliant race. Schumacher is only fifth at the first corner, but he cuts through the opposition and hunts down Hakkinen. Coulthard's engine failure is all the incentive he needs to perform a classic Schumacher passing manoeuvre at the chicane. He is not seen again by his rivals until they bump into him on the podium.

grosser warsteiner preis von

luxemburg

hakkinen drives the
race of his life to
silence the fans and
put himself on pole
position for the title
showdown in japan

Flying Finn: If Mika had ever
driven better in his grand prix
days (left), no one could remember
when. He celebrated by going into
a bizarre post-race dance ritual
(above left) which has put him in
line for a job in Covent Garden
during the close season. Ferrari's
master strategist Ross Brawn
(above right) couldn't believe it:
Schumacher had
been beaten fair and square
in a straight fight.

It must have been all of lap two when a press room cynic put down his pen and announced, "Well, that's that then. See you Michael."

And so it looked. Mika Hakkinen – apparently a virtual dead cert for the world title since March – now had but a distant view of Michael Schumacher's fleeing Ferrari and, worse, he was separated from his arch-rival by a second flash of scarlet. Eddie Irvine had led most of the opening lap of the Luxembourg GP (which, naturally, takes place at Germany's Nürburgring, not half an hour from Schuey's home town of Kerpen), but when the Ulsterman ran wide at the Veedol chicane his team leader nipped through the gap and was gone. If it was another piece of deliberate self-sacrifice by Irvine, it was subtly done.

The massive crowd certainly couldn't foresee anything other than a Ferrari victory – and many of them couldn't see very much at all. They had been up all night, carousing in the bars and on the camp sites after Schumacher and Irvine snaffled up the front row on Saturday afternoon. The biggest threat to their hero could conceivably have been lack of sleep, given that he was staying at the circuit hotel and the barrage of rockets had lasted for as long as the revellers were still capable of finding the fuse.

But as the scarlet flags waved and yet more beer frothed into ever-receptive steins, Hakkinen was about to spoil the party atmosphere with the drive of his life.

Irvine managed to play the bolshy rear gunner until lap 14, but the Ferrari driver was clearly not comfortable maintaining the pace at which Hakkinen was pushing him and, after a couple of wobbly moments, he succumbed to Mika's pressure when the Finn dived past as they approached the chicane.

It still didn't look like much of a straight fight, mind, because Schumacher was already over eight seconds clear.

But not for long.

Hakkinen recovered five seconds of his deficit over the next 10 laps and he took the lead on lap 25, when Schumacher made the first of his two pit stops. With a clear track

Hakkinen went into overdrive, putting in his quickest three laps of the race and, when he emerged from his own pit stop, five laps later, he was just in front of the Ferrari, which snaked viciously under braking as Schumacher attempted unsuccessfully to unsettle his adversary.

The two title protagonists stayed together until their second and final stops, when McLaren's sharper pit work allowed Hakkinen to extend his hard-earned lead.

On the podium Schumacher's boyish grin had vanished. There was no escaping the fact

> "I think today answers any questions about Mika's ability to deal with Schumacher's challenge"
>
> **Adrian Newey, McLaren designer**

a ring and a prayer

Charge of the flight brigade: Tom Pryce's Shadow demonstrates the challenge of the original Nürburgring in 1975 (above). Today, punters can sample the place for a few quid per lap – but you are unlikely to be able to replicate this in the average hire car.

WHEN THE Nürburgring was opened in 1984 it was slagged off simply for having the temerity to share the same name as the legendary, 14-mile circuit which corkscrews through the neighbouring forestry.

But over the years criticism of the 'new' Nürburgring has cooled. What appeared to be a dull and insipid circuit layout 14 years ago actually comes across as quite imaginative by the standards of the current day. There are third-and-fourth-gear corners and the drivers reckon it is possible to build up a good rhythm.

Much as they quite like it, however, they are quick to point out the paucity of overtaking opportunities – and even quicker to shoot next door given half a chance to sample the Nordschleife, the original Nürburgring.

It is something anyone can do. It doesn't matter whether you are an F1 star in a Mercedes S-Class or a Dutchman towing a caravan behind an Opel Astra, you can access the old 'Ring for about a fiver per lap.

Caution is required – just as it always was. The circuit is packed with expert bikers who know every square millimetre of the concrete by heart. And their geographical expertise is exceeded only by their commitment. If you are going as fast as you can in an Opel Corsa prepared by Avis or Hertz in Cologne, watch out. That faint buzzing you can hear somewhere in the trees will probably zap past you within the next 30 seconds, changing up to sixth as you hit what you think is the braking area.

Activity on the old 'Ring dies down a little when Schuey and his mates are in the area, but during the course of a lesser race weekend it is safe to say that there will be as big a crowd fascinated by tourists and show-offs tackling the old circuit as there will be watching the action on the new.

Formula One first showed real signs of safety consciousness in the Seventies. . . and for those who weren't around at the time it will be hard to conceive that grand prix racing was only lost to the original Nürburgring after Niki Lauda's fiery accident in 1976.

This is the ultimate living museum – and you can experience it yourself for the price of a race programme and a dodgy burger. There's nothing else in the world quite like it.

that he had been beaten fair and square in a straight fight.

"I think today answers any questions about Mika's ability to deal with Schumacher's challenge," said McLaren technical director Adrian Newey. Hakkinen even got a pat on the back for having insisted on a narrower Bridgestone for the weekend; while many had thought his choice to be misguided, it turned out to be an inspired selection for the cooler race conditions which prevailed. Where Schumacher had been the consistent hare in qualifying, Hakkinen was the man with the pace in the race.

"I really thought we could win today, but we just weren't quick enough and I don't know why," said Michael.

And if he thought he wasn't fast enough, spare a thought for the others.

David Coulthard recovered from a modest start to finish third after passing Irvine during the first round of stops. . . but he was still over half a minute in arrears. Irvine took fourth and Heinz-Harald Frentzen was fifth for Williams after a race-long fight with both Benettons. Remarkably, Giancarlo Fisichella's point for the latter was the team's first in six races.

Jacques Villeneuve would probably have led the Williams attack but for faulty refuelling gear which trashed his one-stop strategy, but that was small concern to a Ferrari team that now had five weeks to redress the balance.

"If you finish second and fourth from the front row, something must be wrong," muttered team boss Jean Todt, darkly.

Where's Mika?: Remarkable Hakkinen-free shot shows Frentzen holding off the Benettons during a race-long fight for fifth place (left). As has become customary, the audience barely noticed the second of their compatriots to breach the top six.

Just champion: Williams test driver Juan Pablo Montoya (right) clinched the FIA F3000 title at the Nürburgring – and then did a deal to race in America's Champ Car series because there simply wasn't space for him in F1 in 1999.

junior showtime

AS WELL as being the final European F1 joust of the season, the Nürburgring was the setting for the last act in the FIA F3000 Championship, which according to the sport's governing body is supposed to be the breeding ground for the F1 stars of the future.

Except, of course, that F1 drivers are usually snapped up for one of two reasons, and ability usually takes second place to cash in the final reckoning.

In 1998 the FIA F3000 series allied itself more closely than ever to F1, with eight of the 12 races acting as grand prix curtain-raisers on a Saturday afternoon.

The championship was not settled, as is customary, until the final race and at the Nürburgring Williams test driver Juan Pablo Montoya eventually clinched the crown by driving conservatively to third place behind Gonzalo Rodriguez – the most successful Uruguayan racing driver in history – and rising Danish star Jason Watt.

The Colombian's quest was aided when title rival Nick Heidfeld was relegated to the back of the grid after the West Competition team – a junior arm of McLaren-Mercedes – inadvertently put the wrong kind of fuel in his car. There was no performance advantage; it was a simple mistake.

Once the race was over there was little that any of the leading drivers had left to prove in a training formula – and yet there was simply no space for any of them to move up into F1 (unless they really wanted to chance their reputation in a Minardi). Montoya will move to the United States in 1999, to race in the premier Champ Car series – and Heidfeld is set for another Merc-backed tilt at the F3000 title.

Without the same level of support, however, the rest of a talented bunch can but sit and hope that their efforts will be noticed by someone, somewhere.

And in the current climate, that's some hope.

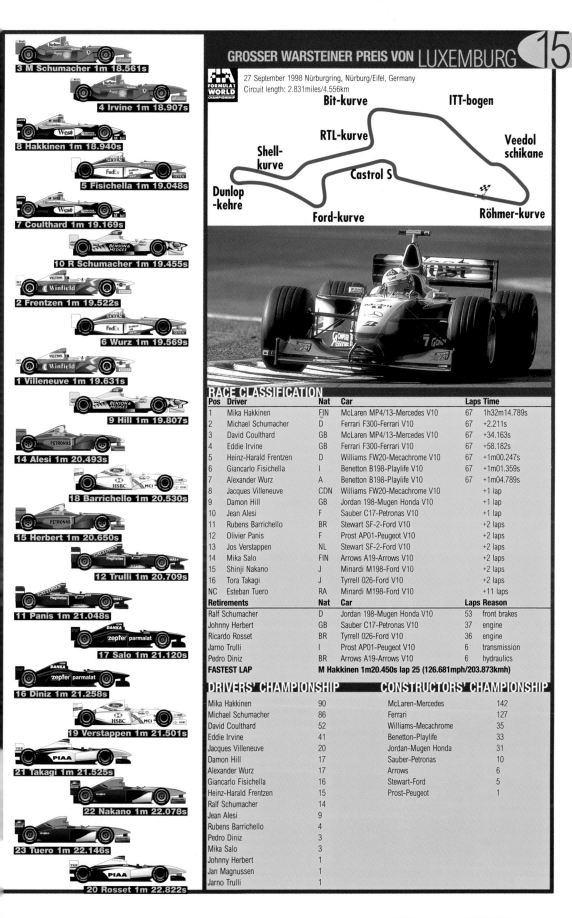

3 M Schumacher 1m 18.561s

4 Irvine 1m 18.907s

8 Hakkinen 1m 18.940s

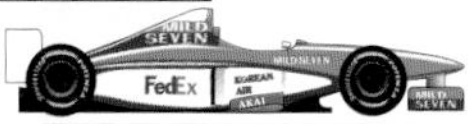
5 Fisichella 1m 19.048s

7 Coulthard 1m 19.169s

10 R Schumacher 1m 19.455s

2 Frentzen 1m 19.522s

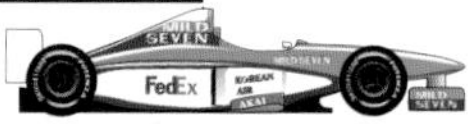
6 Wurz 1m 19.569s

1 Villeneuve 1m 19.631s

9 Hill 1m 19.807s

14 Alesi 1m 20.493s

18 Barrichello 1m 20.530s

15 Herbert 1m 20.650s

12 Trulli 1m 20.709s

11 Panis 1m 21.048s

17 Salo 1m 21.120s

16 Diniz 1m 21.258s

19 Verstappen 1m 21.501s

21 Takagi 1m 21.525s

22 Nakano 1m 22.078s

23 Tuero 1m 22.146s

20 Rosset 1m 22.822s

GROSSER WARSTEINER PREIS VON LUXEMBURG 15

FORMULA 1 WORLD CHAMPIONSHIP

27 September 1998 Nürburgring, Nürburg/Eifel, Germany
Circuit length: 2.831miles/4.556km

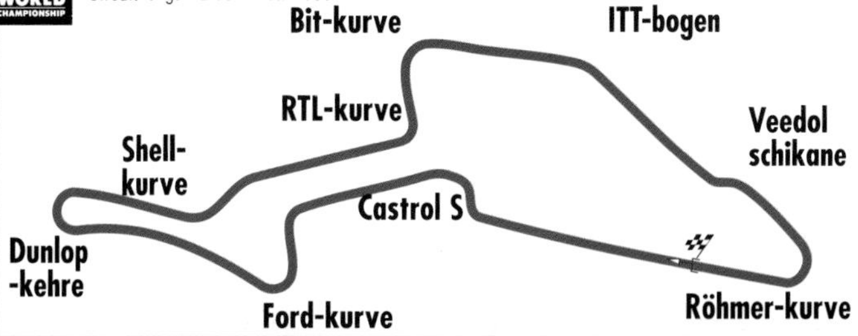

Bit-kurve
ITT-bogen
RTL-kurve
Shell-kurve
Veedol schikane
Castrol S
Dunlop -kehre
Ford-kurve
Röhmer-kurve

RACE CLASSIFICATION

Pos	Driver	Nat	Car	Laps	Time
1	Mika Hakkinen	FIN	McLaren MP4/13-Mercedes V10	67	1h32m14.789s
2	Michael Schumacher	D	Ferrari F300-Ferrari V10	67	+2.211s
3	David Coulthard	GB	McLaren MP4/13-Mercedes V10	67	+34.163s
4	Eddie Irvine	GB	Ferrari F300-Ferrari V10	67	+58.182s
5	Heinz-Harald Frentzen	D	Williams FW20-Mecachrome V10	67	+1m00.247s
6	Giancarlo Fisichella	I	Benetton B198-Playlife V10	67	+1m01.359s
7	Alexander Wurz	A	Benetton B198-Playlife V10	67	+1m04.789s
8	Jacques Villeneuve	CDN	Williams FW20-Mecachrome V10		+1 lap
9	Damon Hill	GB	Jordan 198-Mugen Honda V10		+1 lap
10	Jean Alesi	F	Sauber C17-Petronas V10		+1 lap
11	Rubens Barrichello	BR	Stewart SF-2-Ford V10		+2 laps
12	Olivier Panis	F	Prost AP01-Peugeot V10		+2 laps
13	Jos Verstappen	NL	Stewart SF-2-Ford V10		+2 laps
14	Mika Salo	FIN	Arrows A19-Arrows V10		+2 laps
15	Shinji Nakano	J	Minardi M198-Ford V10		+2 laps
16	Tora Takagi	J	Tyrrell 026-Ford V10		+2 laps
NC	Esteban Tuero	RA	Minardi M198-Ford V10		+11 laps

Retirements	Nat	Car	Laps	Reason
Ralf Schumacher	D	Jordan 198-Mugen Honda V10	53	front brakes
Johnny Herbert	GB	Sauber C17-Petronas V10	37	engine
Ricardo Rosset	BR	Tyrrell 026-Ford V10	36	engine
Jarno Trulli	I	Prost AP01-Peugeot V10	6	transmission
Pedro Diniz	BR	Arrows A19-Arrows V10	6	hydraulics

FASTEST LAP **M Hakkinen 1m20.450s lap 25 (126.681mph/203.873kmh)**

DRIVERS' CHAMPIONSHIP

Mika Hakkinen	90
Michael Schumacher	86
David Coulthard	52
Eddie Irvine	41
Jacques Villeneuve	20
Damon Hill	17
Alexander Wurz	17
Giancarlo Fisichella	16
Heinz-Harald Frentzen	15
Ralf Schumacher	14
Jean Alesi	9
Rubens Barrichello	4
Pedro Diniz	3
Mika Salo	3
Johnny Herbert	1
Jan Magnussen	1
Jarno Trulli	1

CONSTRUCTORS' CHAMPIONSHIP

McLaren-Mercedes	142
Ferrari	127
Williams-Mecachrome	35
Benetton-Playlife	33
Jordan-Mugen Honda	31
Sauber-Petronas	10
Arrows	6
Stewart-Ford	5
Prost-Peugeot	1

pride for hakkinen came after schumacher's stall as the world's best drivers took three attempts to get the final race of the year under way

The long way home: Schuey ambles back to contemplate a third successive winter without a world champion's trophy on his mantelpiece in Lausanne (above). Jet flagged: Hakkinen smokes to a halt in front of the ecstatic McLaren team after cruising home to become Finland's second F1 champion. The country has some way to go before its motor racing roll of honour matches its ski-jumping record.

fuji television
japanese
grand prix

It was billed as the showdown to end all showdowns: eager pretender (Mika Hakkinen) versus wily former champ (Michael Schumacher); perfectionism (McLaren) against passion (Ferrari); Britain takes on Italy.

Yet it was over before it had even begun.

The Japanese GP should have been a brilliant race waged between drivers and teams on top form. Qualifying, where Schumacher snatched pole from Hakkinen, only added to the anticipation. But it all went horribly, horribly wrong for Ferrari.

After an aborted first start Schumacher hit trouble at the second attempt and stalled after a clutch malfunction. His punishment – relegation to the back of the grid – effectively trashed his hopes before the start.

It was a crushing blow after five weeks of solid preparation, during which Ferrari had even gone to the trouble of flooding its Mugello test track to prepare for the eventuality of a wet race.

The Ferrari man needed to win with Hakkinen lower than second. But the McLaren driver immediately established a comfortable lead over Eddie Irvine, the Ulsterman for once given his head and told to push for all he was worth.

"We discussed tactics before the race, but none of them included Michael starting from the back," groaned Eddie. His was a fine drive, but Hakkinen was always in control.

although he did enough to rise as high as third ahead of david coulthard, ferrari's title pretender was on borrowed time

spark of a champion

SOME people find it hard to warm to Mika Hakkinen. He doesn't give many interviews and in post-race press conferences he usually appears uncommunicative and disinterested.

Cosseted in the ranks of the McLaren team since 1993, he has learned well that speaking his mind in public does not go down well with his masters.

But it is not fair to slate the 30-year-old Finn for his perceived reticence. The English language does not help his cause and neither does the all-consuming joy of winning grands prix after years of struggle. Before October 1997 Hakkinen had competed in 100-odd, led several and triumphed in none. Yet by the time Japan was over he had won nine: all year, he had been adjusting to the shock of his dreams coming true. And that was particularly true in Suzuka, where he was stunned by his title triumph.

"I don't really know what to feel yet," he said. "I remember being here in 1996 when Damon Hill was winning his championship. We were talking in the scrutineering bay and he said, 'One day you are going to do it'. I just said, 'Yeah, yeah'.

"He was sitting there telling me what he was feeling and I couldn't say much. Now I can understand what he felt like.

"Since I started in Formula One in 1991 it has been a fight every year as I tried to maximise my results personally and for my team. Since I joined this team in 1993 I continued the effort to win races, but it took a long time. Now that it has happened, and looking back over all that time, we can be happy."

Never had Hakkinen more cause to fight than in 1995, when a sickening accident in practice at Adelaide left him critically ill. His rapid recovery to take the grid for the next Australian race six months later was one of F1's great stories. And now, as world champion, he had become another.

For those who still think Hakkinen is taciturn and unemotional, witness his behaviour as he was being escorted to the podium after the race. Breaking free of his minders, he legged it through parc fermé towards the grandstands to wave back at a legion of cheering spectators.

It was the only time he put a foot wrong all weekend.

Stall story: The world's media descend on Schumacher shortly before his basic error.

All over the Hill: Schumacher sped through the field to reach the outer extremities of the top six – and then found Damon in resolute form (above left).

Scrap mettle: Not only did Hill fend off Schumacher, he also outfumbled Frentzen in the end after following his future team-mate for much of the afternoon (below left).

Joys R Us: Hakkinen celebrates the fact that he can now go home and catch some serious ice hockey action on TV (top).

As ever, Schumacher grabbed the attention, passing cars right, left and centre until he came across Damon Hill's sixth-placed Jordan. There he sat as his old enemy refused to give way and he only moved forward when Hill made his first pit stop. "I think he was more concerned with keeping me behind him than anything else," grumbled Schumacher.

Although he did enough to rise as high as third ahead of David Coulthard, Ferrari's title pretender was on borrowed time. On lap 31, his right rear tyre exploded after he had run over accident debris from a clash between Esteban Tuero and Toranosuke Takagi, who thus unwittingly made their biggest impact of the season.

"It's disappointing, but I don't feel too bad," said Schumacher. "We didn't lose the title

a bang and a whimper

Debris from the shunt between Takagi (right) and Tuero caused Schuey's blow-out season (below right).

Brit by Brit: Coulthard and Irvine head for a combined seasonal total of 17 podium finishes.

FORMULA One bade farewell to two of its oldest names in Suzuka – although both would doubtless have preferred to bow out on a different note.

Japan finally marked the end of the road for the Tyrrell team, thrice world champion with Jackie Stewart in the past but gradually absorbed by new owner British American Racing from the start of the season.

Founder Ken Tyrrell was only an occasional observer during the last year of the team which bears his name and the 73-year-old had to watch a disappointing campaign in the mould of his team's more recent history.

The last Tyrrell, the 026, plainly had plenty of promise – rookie Tora Takagi proved it by outqual-

here, we lost it at the beginning of the season. We should be proud of what we've done since."

Hakkinen, eyeing the stricken Ferrari, knew it was all over, and was left to battle only his wandering concentration. "I was almost whistling to myself in the car for the last 10 laps," he admitted, "but [boss] Ron Dennis came on the radio and told me to be cool." He was.

If Hill had been satisfied to keep Schumacher behind, it was nothing to the sense of elation within the Jordan team after Damon mugged future team-mate Heinz-Harald Frentzen's Williams to nick fourth place two corners from the end. That was more than enough for his team to beat Benetton to fourth in the constructors' standings, and kick off the kind of party for which Alka Seltzer should be standard issue on the door. But it was nothing compared to the celebration already underway at McLaren. . .

ifying Ford's works team Stewart on several occasions – but the inexperienced Japanese faded badly in races. Partner Ricardo Rosset never got to grips with things and failed to qualify on several occasions.

Technical chief Harvey Postlethwaite, who took over as MD from Tyrrell, summed it up thus: "In a way we are pleased it is finally all over. Having to participate instead of compete has not been easy and sometimes it causes a rage which is difficult to contain."

You could see his point in Suzuka. Rosset failed to beat the 107 per cent cut off to make it onto the grid. And sole representative Takagi became embroiled in a daft dust-up with Esteban Tuero which left both on the sidelines. What a way to go.

Ironically, however, Tyrrell did play a part in deciding the world championship as Goodyear faced up to quitting F1 on a rare losing note.

The Akron tyre giant, a veteran of 451 victories and every world title since 1984, had tested ceaselessly with Ferrari to develop the perfect rubber for Bridgestone's home track. It had clearly done an excellent job too – until the charging Schumacher ran over the debris from the Tuero/Takagi collision.

The ensuing explosion not only extinguished the German's slim hopes, it was also a sad end to a final season in which Goodyear – reeling from Bridgestone's early-season strength – had done absolutely everything it could to go out with a bang.

Unfortunately, this wasn't quite what it had in mind.

3 M Schumacher 1m 36.293s

8 Hakkinen 1m 36.471s

7 Coulthard 1m 37.496s

4 Irvine 1m 38.197s

2 Frentzen 1m 38.272s

1 Villeneuve 1m 38.448s

10 R Schumacher 1m 38.461s

9 Hill 1m 38.603s

6 Wurz 1m 38.959s

5 Fisichella 1m 39.080s

15 Herbert 1m 39.234s

14 Alesi 1m 39.448s

11 Panis 1m 40.037s

12 Trulli 1m 40.111s

17 Salo 1m 40.387s

18 Barrichello 1m 40.502s

21 Takagi 1m 40.619s

16 Diniz 1m 40.687s

19 Verstappen 1m 40.943s

22 Nakano 1m 41.315s

23 Tuero 1m 42.358s

DID NOT QUALIFY
20 Rosset BR
Tyrrell 026-Ford V10 1m 43.259s

FORMULA 1 WORLD CHAMPIONSHIP

1 November 1998 Suzuka Circuit International Racing Course, Ino-Cho, Suzuka-City
Circuit length: 3.644miles/5.864km

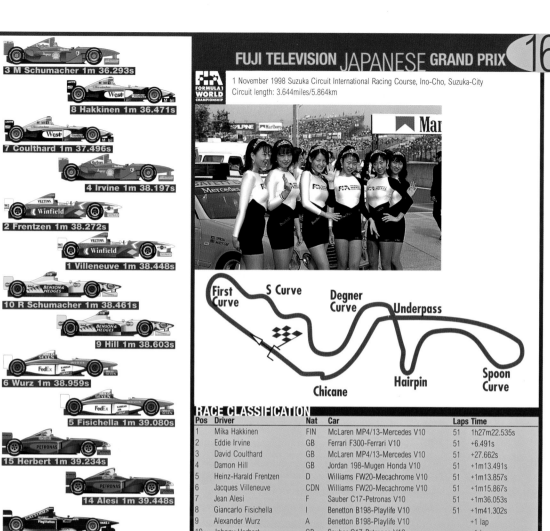

First Curve — S Curve — Degner Curve — Underpass — Spoon Curve — Hairpin — Chicane

RACE CLASSIFICATION

Pos	Driver	Nat	Car	Laps	Time
1	Mika Hakkinen	FIN	McLaren MP4/13-Mercedes V10	51	1h27m22.535s
2	Eddie Irvine	GB	Ferrari F300-Ferrari V10	51	+6.491s
3	David Coulthard	GB	McLaren MP4/13-Mercedes V10	51	+27.662s
4	Damon Hill	GB	Jordan 198-Mugen Honda V10	51	+1m13.491s
5	Heinz-Harald Frentzen	D	Williams FW20-Mecachrome V10	51	+1m13.857s
6	Jacques Villeneuve	CDN	Williams FW20-Mecachrome V10	51	+1m15.867s
7	Jean Alesi	F	Sauber C17-Petronas V10	51	+1m36.053s
8	Giancarlo Fisichella	I	Benetton B198-Playlife V10	51	+1m41.302s
9	Alexander Wurz	A	Benetton B198-Playlife V10		+1 lap
10	Johnny Herbert	GB	Sauber C17-Petronas V10		+1 lap
11	Olivier Panis	F	Prost AP01-Peugeot V10		+1 lap
12	Jarno Trulli	I	Prost AP01B-Peugeot V10		+3 laps

Retirements	Nat	Car	Laps	Reason
Shinji Nakano	J	Minardi M198-Ford V10	40	
Michael Schumacher	D	Ferrari F300-Ferrari V10	31	rear puncture
Tora Takagi	J	Tyrrell 026-Ford V10	28	accident
Esteban Tuero	RA	Minardi M198-Ford V10	28	accident
Rubens Barrichello	BR	Stewart SF-2-Ford V10	25	hydraulics
Jos Verstappen	NL	Stewart SF-2-Ford V10	21	gearbox
Mika Salo	FIN	Arrows A19-Arrows V10	14	hydraulic leak
Ralf Schumacher	D	Jordan 198-Mugen Honda V10	13	engine
Pedro Diniz	BR	Arrows A19-Arrows V10	2	spin
FASTEST LAP		M Schumacher, 1m40.190s lap 19 (130.925mph/210.704kmh)		

DRIVERS' CHAMPIONSHIP

Mika Hakkinen	100
Michael Schumacher	86
David Coulthard	56
Eddie Irvine	47
Jacques Villeneuve	21
Damon Hill	20
Heinz-Harald Frentzen	17
Alexander Wurz	17
Giancarlo Fisichella	16
Ralf Schumacher	14
Jean Alesi	9
Rubens Barrichello	4
Pedro Diniz	3
Mika Salo	3
Johnny Herbert	1
Jan Magnussen	1
Jarno Trulli	1

CONSTRUCTORS' CHAMPIONSHIP

McLaren-Mercedes	156
Ferrari	133
Williams-Mecachrome	38
Jordan-Mugen Honda	34
Benetton-Playlife	33
Sauber-Petronas	10
Arrows	6
Stewart-Ford	5
Prost-Peugeot	1

this was the
year
that was
how mclaren, mercedes and bridgestone combined to leave a conspicuous hole in the schumacher family trophy cabinet. and lots of other stuff

We should be thankful to Ferrari for sharpening up its act. This year its technical department hardly acted as fast as its prize asset can drive, but at least it did enough to allow Michael Schumacher to breathe some belated life into the world title contest.

That said, McLaren and Mercedes merit a degree of gratitude for building something which was technically superior without being bullet-proof. Between them Mika Hakkinen and David Coulthard were in a winning position at some stage during every grand prix weekend; that McLaren was defeated on

Flying start: Hakkinen is swamped by the media – even though he's done no more than take pole position for the first race of the year at this juncture in the campaign (above).

Crush helmet: Schumacher is utterly devastated (left) to learn that Bayer Leverkusen have been knocked out of the UEFA Cup by Rangers. Either that or he can't believe that Damon Hill has just won a race in a Jordan.

Gongs of the Year

TOP 10 DRIVERS

1 **Mika Hakkinen** (above)
He deserves it because of that Nürburgring performance
2 **Michael Schumacher**
It's too easy just to put him number one, even if he is really
3 **Eddie Irvine**
For obedience beyond the call of duty
4 **David Coulthard**
Top bloke, but didn't win enough in best car
5 **Damon Hill**
For waking up in the second half of the year
6 **Jacques Villeneuve**
Performed much better than his car all season
7 **Jean Alesi** (right)
Strangely more impressive in a Sauber than he was in a Benetton
8 **Giancarlo Fisichella**
Fast and promising, though racecraft is sometimes flawed
9 **Ralf Schumacher**
Not as good as his brother, but probably better than you are
10 **Alexander Wurz**
For outstanding calmness in the face of outstanding accidents

it was pleasant, too, that they engaged in battle without any of the rancour which has marred so many confrontations in recent seasons

not to deny Hakkinen the full merit of his world title.

Just over a year after he had taken the first F1 victory of his career at Jerez (deserved, albeit not in the manner it was clumsily gift-wrapped), the Finn roared to his ninth grand prix triumph to wrap up a championship which, frankly, had looked destined to be his almost from the moment Coulthard sportingly waved him past in Melbourne.

Sure, he had the best car, but there was more to his success than that. The finest illustration was at the penultimate race of the year, on Schumacher's home turf at the Nürburgring. For the very first time the momentum was with the German, who had bludgeoned his way level on points before the race.

Happy happy shake: The scrap between Hakkinen and Schumacher was one of the most harmonious in recent seasons (above left), without the slightest flicker of a bicker.

seven occasions was due to human and mechanical fallibility, Schumacher's belligerence (in Argentina), Ferrari's tactical brilliance (Hungary) and the weather (Spa). Only in France did Ferrari win a straight fight where strategy did not have a significant influence on the outcome.

For all his perceived flaws as a sportsman (and his anti-Coulthard tirade in Belgium was inexcusable, no matter how you dress it up), few would deny that Schumacher has a greater ability than his rivals to get more from the machinery at his disposal. But that is

Gongs of the Year

MOST DRUNKEN FANS

1 The Germans in Austria
2 The Germans in Germany
3 The Germans in Luxembourg (which is, in fact, Germany)
4 The Germans in Hungary
5 The Germans in Belgium

Gongs of the Year
BEST CARS
1 McLaren MP4-13
2 Just about everything else

schumacher, regarded as the best in the business, has now had to sit and watch as the last three world championships have gone elsewhere

When the Ferraris swept up the front row in qualifying the naysayers gathered in force and predicted that Hakkinen's unfamiliarity with chasing world titles would lead him to crack.

He responded by driving better than ever, beating his arch-rival in a straight fight and confirming that this was a battle between two men who could justly have laid claim to be the best in the world.

It was pleasant, too, that they engaged in battle without any of the rancour which has marred so many confrontations in recent seasons. There were some spectacular rows during the course of the campaign, but none brought the two main protagonists face to face in animosity. Their mutual respect was tangible and their handshakes before and after the Suzuka finale were unusually sincere by motor racing standards. Schumacher, regarded as the best in the business, has now

had to sit and watch as the last three world championships have gone elsewhere and Ferrari, which feels as though it has been promising it will win a title "next year" almost since Alberto Ascari was a lad, announced as much – again – within five minutes of the chequered flag falling at Suzuka.

Hakkinen's emergence as Finland's second world champion (after his mentor, Keke Rosberg, who needed to win only once to do the job in 1982) earned him Schumacher's utmost admiration and left his own team-mate with plenty to think about.

In each of the previous two years Coulthard had outscored his McLaren partner – so it was ironic that he should score fewer wins this season, when he had an equipment advantage, than he did when he was against

Home, sweet home: Within a cocktail cherry's throw of his adopted residence, Hakkinen's Monaco triumph (top) was easy for a bloke who used to make winning appear so difficult.

The great smell of brutes: Hakkinen and Schuey compare deodorant performance in France (above left).

Gongs of the Year
After You Claude Award for generosity to team-mate
David Coulthard in Melbourne (below). Eddie Irvine absolutely everywhere

superior Williams and Ferrari opposition in 1997. He had his fair share of mechanical misfortune, true, and can claim that circumstances beyond his control cost him probable victories in Argentina, Canada, Germany and Italy. And Hakkinen still owes him a favour for the Scot's act of rare sportsmanship in Australia. Racing driver keeps promise: there's a story.

By the second half of the year Coulthard came to accept that it was logical he should play a supporting role as Hakkinen faced a

Gongs of the Year

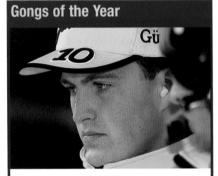

MOST IMPROVED DRIVER
Ralf Schumacher – who went from accident waiting to happen to star in the making in the space of a five-race mid-season purple patch

growing challenge from Schumacher, but during the year as a whole his reputation took something of a knock and a flying start is required in 1999 if he is to change the thinking of a new breed of doubter which has appeared in the paddock.

At least Coulthard knows he will start the new season with a chance of winning races. It will take a mixture of circumstances before that becomes a possibility for Eddie Irvine, who remains – on the surface – happy to tow the Ferrari party line and drive principally for his team-mate's benefit. Still, he is well rewarded for doing so and, as he basks in the wealth of his pastime, he can reflect on the best season of his career. The fact that he climbed the podium steps in half the races hinted at a previously unseen level of consistency. And he usually wasn't too far from Schumacher in terms of qualifying speed, either.

> it is not uncommon for reigning champions to have a duff follow-up season, but villeneuve realised he could kiss his crown goodbye in melbourne

Mint tactics: Ferrari scored its most spectacular success in Hungary (top), where inspired strategy and a bloke who is capable of driving at qualifying speed all day long conjured up an unlikely victory.

With the exception of Damon Hill's stunning Spa win for Jordan, the rest had to make do with mere scraps.

It is not uncommon for reigning champions to have a duff follow-up season, but Jacques Villeneuve realised he could kiss his crown good-bye after the opening qualifying session in Melbourne. The Canadian was left floundering after Williams' technical department was revealed to have spent the winter in hibernation. The team improved slowly during the year, though a first winless season since 1988 was always odds-on. Villeneuve had to wait until the 11th race at Hockenheim before he managed a top three finish, though his consistent ability to edge into the top six at least gave him enough points to pip Hill to fifth place in the final standings.

Damon spent the first few months of the year wondering what the hell he had done committing to Jordan for two years – but such was the team's rate of recovery that it went on to pip Benetton for fourth overall in the constructors' championship, its best-ever performance.

Ralf Schumacher did more than his fair

benetton's laudable youth policy

Gongs of the Year

RORY BREMNER AWARD FOR BEST IMPERSONATION OF A WORLD TITLE RIVAL
Mika Hakkinen, who out-Schumachered Michael Schumacher with his brilliant third-to-first drive at the Nürburgring

share to assist Jordan, too, but for all that he was impressive at Silverstone, Hockenheim, Spa and elsewhere, he was still prone to bizarre lapses of judgment.

Some predict a rough road for him in the strait-laced world of Williams, but he will have to go some to fare worse than Heinz-Harald Frentzen, who for two years has been sadly miscast in his supposed role as a miracle replacement for Hill. The German, largely inconspicuous when he had the best car on the planet the previous year, actually rediscovered some of his gusto this season. But the fact that the team had taken a step backwards left him pretty much where he started.

Benetton's laudable youth policy ultimately failed to pay dividends as the team vanished from the radar screen in the second part of

benetton's laudable youth policy ultimately failed to pay dividends as the team vanished from the radar screen in the second part of the year

Crash of the titans: Damon Hill leads at Spa (top) as Hakkinen and Schumacher are in the process of driving into each other in civilised, non-argumentative fashion.

the year. And such was new boss David Richards' frustration with the lack of progress that he took it upon himself to become the old boss before the year was out. Even so, Giancarlo Fisichella could have won in Canada and Alexander Wurz showed that he had learned a bit from his dad Franz's European Rallycross background with his stubborn, physical resistance of Schumacher Snr in

Gongs of the Year

BEST OVERTAKING MANOEUVRE
Michael Schumacher on Damon Hill at Spa

MOST EXPENSIVE OVERTAKING MANOEUVRE
Giancarlo Fisichella (below) on Shinji Nakano at Spa

Monaco. But the fact remains that the team is currently plunging down the pecking order and the end-of-season management discontent risks accelerating the decline of the operation which won back-to-back titles in 1994/95.

Jean Alesi managed to squeeze enough out of a Sauber to rekindle reminders of much that had been forgotten while he was at

Gongs of the Year

BEST DRIVES
Michael Schumacher in Hungary. Mika Hakkinen at the Nürburgring. Damon Hill in Belgium

WORST DRIVE
Ricardo Rosset's (below) failure to qualify in Monaco after pranging the guardrail as he attempted a three-point turn

Never say dye: It was a year to forget for reigning world champion Jacques Villeneuve (admiring the local architecture in Monte Carlo, above). The Canadian changed the colour of his hair more frequently than he appeared on the podium.

Benetton. It won him the undying affection of the Swiss team (a catalyst for Johnny Herbert's departure from the fold), but only in the once-a-decade freak conditions we saw at Spa is the most experienced F1 racer in the pack likely to have any chance of adding to his solitary grand prix win.

Stewart found its second year tough and sacking scapegoat Jan Magnussen in mid-season made little difference; not that the team had expected it to be easy. Prost found it even harder, and given the high national expectation of its partnership with Peugeot that was a crushing blow. The French team started off on the wrong foot with a gearbox whose complexity made the BRM V16 look like a paper plane. Not only that, it didn't work terribly well.

Arrows' introduction of its own Brian Hart-designed V10 was always doomed to be problematic without the funds to develop it and, talking of meagre budgets, Minardi and Tyrrell did all that could be expected within their means.

With Tyrrell's absorption into the new British American Racing set-up, there is a danger that Minardi won't have anyone at all to play with next season. Chances are, however, that it will only be the Italian team's drivers who actually notice.

143

The rest of the Gongs of the Year

MERYL STREEP AWARD FOR POST-RACE DRAMATICS

Michael Schumacher – who claimed that both Damon Hill and David Coulthard tried to kill him during the season

BIGGEST SURPRISE

Esteban Tuero not being anything like as inept as had been predicted

BIGGEST DISAPPOINTMENTS

The Williams FW20 – not what the doctor ordered for the world champion constructor. The Prost-Peugeot alliance – new national dream team proved to be decidedly mediocre. At least France could take solace from success in other sporting contests during the summer

THE CAPTAIN SCARLET AWARD FOR INDESTRUCTIBILITY

Benetton's Alexander Wurz – for getting involved in two brain-rattling shunts in as many grands prix (Monaco and Canada) – and then acting as though nothing had happened. He even took the team spare to fourth place after his barrel-roll in Montreal

THE LIVERPOOL FC PRIZE FOR PERSISTENT UNDERACHIEVEMENT

Jointly awarded to Williams and Benetton for their spectacular failure to match former glories

BIGGEST COCK-UP

The administrative disaster that led to Michael Schumacher winning the British Grand Prix without taking the chequered flag. It cost the crowd any idea of what was going on and the stewards their jobs

THE STONE ROSES DIFFICULT SECOND ALBUM AWARD

Prost Grand Prix, for its nightmare year with a squad rebuilt to Alain Prost's specification

THE RON DAVIES AWARD FOR BEING IN THE WRONG PLACE AT THE WRONG TIME

David Coulthard, Spa. (Actually, over half the field probably qualified for this in Belgium)

THE VIAGRA TROPHY

To Damon Hill, the oldest man in the field with the biggest spring in his step at Spa

THE PETER MANDELSON/MILLENNIUM DOME AWARD FOR STRUCTURES NO ONE WANTS

To whichever designer first came up with the now-banned X-wings (step forward Mike Gascoyne, late of Tyrrell and now at Jordan)

THE BILL CLINTON AWARD FOR NOT HAVING A RELATIONSHIP WITH SOMEONE CLOSE BY

To Jean Alesi and Johnny Herbert

BEST IMPERSONATION OF SYLVESTER STALLONE

Michael Schumacher for his pit lane tantrum at Spa

WORST IMPERSONATION OF SYLVESTER STALLONE

Sylvester Stallone, who didn't take up a trip in the McLaren two-seater at Silverstone (the official excuse was that he didn't have time to do the medical, though it was alleged that it might not be good PR should Rambo be seen feeling a tad woozy in public)

THE GINGER SPICE FIGURINE FOR GOING YOUR OWN WAY

To Ken Tyrrell (left) and (ex-) Benetton boss David Richards

THE GEORGE GRAHAM AWARD FOR SUCCUMBING TO GRASS WHICH APPEARS TO BE GREENER ON THE OTHER SIDE

To Ralf Schumacher

THE MARTIN O'NEILL PRIZE FOR KNOWING THAT THE GRASS IS GREENER ON THE OTHER SIDE BUT STAYING PUT ANYWAY

To Rubens Barrichello

THE RICHARD BRANSON PRIZE FOR GARNERING PUBLICITY

To Jordan, which had a succession of guests of the calibre of Ryan Giggs and Emma Noble at the start of the season, so that photographers took pictures of something other than a car which, at the time, was absolutely useless